D0849293

Just for Starters

Just for Starters

A Treasury of 350 of the
World's Best Hors d'Oeuvres and Appetizers

Gloria Edwinn

The Viking Press
New York

Copyright © Gloria Edwinn, 1981
All rights reserved
First published in 1981 by The Viking Press
625 Madison Avenue, New York, N.Y. 10022
Published simultaneously in Canada by
Penguin Books Canada Limited

Library of Congress Cataloging in Publication Data
Edwinn, Gloria
   Just for starters.
   Includes index.
   1.   Cookery (Appetizers)   I.   Title.
TX740.E38   641.8'12   80-51771
ISBN 0-670-41093-4

Printed in the United States of America
Set in Linotype Century Schoolbook
Drawings by Carol Ann Robson

Grateful acknowledgment is made to the following for permission to re-
print copyrighted material:

Atheneum Publishers, Inc., and John Schaffner Associates, Inc.: "Onion
     Rings" from *Cool Entertaining* by Irma Rhode. Copyright © 1976
     by Irma Rhode.
Harper & Row, Publishers, Inc.: "Salmon Mousse" (blender method)
     from *The New York Times Menu Cookbook* by Craig Claiborne.
     Copyright © 1966 by The New York Times Company.
Hawthorn Books, a Division of Elsevier-Dutton Publishing Co., Inc.,
     and John Schaffner Associates, Inc.: "Deep Fried Eggplant Batter"
     from *Florence Lin's Chinese Vegetarian Cookbook* by Florence Lin.
     Copyright © 1976 by Florence S. Lin.
Maurice Moore-Betty: "Vegetarian Antipasto" from *Cooking for Oc-
     casions* by Maurice Moore-Betty. Copyright © 1970 by Maurice
     Moore-Betty.

To the memory of my mother and father, who thought that being able to cook was more important than learning Middle English. This book would not have been possible without the patience of my husband and the cooperation of his stomach.

Contents

Introduction

For many people, cooking is a joy rather than a chore; for me, it is a consuming passion. Over many years, I have reveled in dreaming up new dishes and watching the gratifying reactions of my family and friends.

Of all the facets of cooking, hors d'oeuvres are my favorite. They are different from other kinds of food. You can experiment without taking the costly chance that you do with a $20 roast. Today's prices may discourage one from using shrimp, lobster, or crab as the basic ingredient of a main dish, but as hors d'oeuvres, where a relatively small quantity is needed, they are still within reason. I find, too, that guests are more willing to be adventuresome about tasting exotic fare in bite-sized portions. Besides, hors d'oeuvres are a challenge to my own palate. They are more assertively seasoned than most other foods, and each one must stand alone instead of relating to other dishes in the same course. There is no need to worry about clashing sauces or colors, since conflicting foods probably won't be on the plate at the same time.

Organizing a cocktail party is more demanding than planning a three-course dinner, since there will probably be more individual items to prepare and serve. I try to pick as many dishes as possible that can be prepared in advance, and refrigerated or frozen. This leaves me time to garnish the serving platters so that the food looks as good as it tastes.

If I am serving hors d'oeuvres as a prelude to dinner, I keep the quantity down so that the appetizers tease but do not ruin the appetite. Three well-chosen items will usually suffice. I avoid repeating ingredients or flavors that will appear in the dinner to follow. I might serve a cheese, a vegetable, and a meat or fish, perhaps one of them hot. When I invite people for cocktails only, the hors d'oeuvres are heartier, more varied, and more numerous. Relieved of the necessity of preparing dinner, I can produce more elaborate concoctions. However, the principle of diversification still holds: don't bore your public by serving two spreads with a cream-cheese base.

Although a cocktail party offers the temptation to show off one's culinary versatility, it is unwise to serve more than two hot hors d'oeuvres; and at least one of these should be something that can be kept hot in a chafing dish throughout the party. Whatever the menu, remember that overambition interferes with peace of mind and reduces the amount of time for enjoying oneself. Unless I am serving only a few people, I choose for hot hors d'oeuvres only foods that will be able to stand constant heat for an hour or more. For these it is necessary to have a sauce as an insulator.

It is almost impossible to specify precisely the number of servings you can expect from a given quantity of hors d'oeuvres. This varies according to whether you are planning a predinner teaser or a full-scale cocktail party. With hors d'oeuvres that are individual tidbits or finger foods such as shrimps, mushrooms, or turnovers, allow one or two for each guest. With dips and spreads, two cups of a mixture should yield about twenty servings. (Of course, if the guests are enthusiastic about a dish, it will disappear sooner!)

Assuming that the reader does not have a staff of kitchen helpers and must function as greeter as well as cook, I have included chiefly recipes for dishes that are relatively easy both to prepare and serve. I have omitted hors d'oeuvres that require painstaking serving techniques and emphasized finger foods and self-help spreads and dips, ruling out plates and forks whenever possible. In the instructions I have indicated whether a recipe can be prepared in advance, and how long the dish can be kept in the refrigerator, and have given techniques for dishes that can be frozen.

When the last guest has departed, the aftermath should not be stacks of soggy canapés that must be chucked straight into the garbage can. Most leftover spreads and dips can be re-

refrigerated, although not refrozen. Leftover hot hors d'oeuvres may provide an elegant dinner the next evening. (It is often a good idea to have a small informal party the night after a big party.) If you have no leftovers and are faced with unexpected guests, the section on emergency measures should be consulted.

Above all, a cocktail party or hors d'oeuvre course should call forth all your inventiveness, whimsy, and boldness, and with the recipes in this book I have tried to provide the stimulus of novel ideas and unexpected combinations. While certain universal favorites could not be omitted, to most of these I have added flavor or texture innovations representing the versions that over the years I have found the most successful.

Notes for Using This Book

Whenever butter is specified, unsalted (sweet) butter is meant. Except in pastry dough, unsalted margarine can be substituted. To melt butter, cut it in small pieces instead of using large chunks; it will melt faster and is less likely to burn.

Sour-cream substitutes, lower in calories, can be made by draining yogurt or creaming low-fat cottage cheese; see index for recipes.

Homemade mayonnaise is strongly recommended for any recipe in which mayonnaise is called for; see index.

Egg whites will have more volume if beaten at room temperature.

When salt is specified I mean kosher salt; if you use regular salt you may need a little less. Quantities of salt and pepper are a matter of personal preference; those given are merely a guide. With food to be served cold, increase the salt; chilling tends to deaden flavor.

Fresh herbs, when available, are almost always preferable to dried, even home-dried. I am fortunate in having an herb garden, but many kinds can be grown on a sunny windowsill. However, I usually specify dried herbs because fresh ones are sometimes impossible to obtain when you need them. In general, 1 teaspoon of dried herbs is equivalent to 1 tablespoon fresh. Always crush dried herbs in your fingers before adding them; this brings out the flavor. When using in cold dishes, soak the herb at least 10 minutes in some of the liquid used in the dish. Unfortunately jars or packages of herbs are so large that the herb often loses its flavor before the package is used up; the only solution is to buy a new package. In cooking I always use the flat-leaved Italian parsley, which has infinitely more flavor, using the curly variety only for decoration. Avoid frozen or fresh-dried chives; they are flavorless. If fresh are not available, substitute the green tops of scallions, chopped very fine.

Garlic, onions, and scallions vary greatly in size, and to some extent, in strength of flavor. In these recipes a clove of garlic means a medium-sized clove, which, when minced or crushed, usually makes about ½ teaspoon. If cloves are very large or very small, you may need to measure the chopped amount. The easiest way to remove the skin from a clove of garlic is to smash it on a flat surface with a heavy implement such as a meat pounder or a cleaver.

Onions are specified by size or by the quantity of chopped onion needed. An average-sized shallot, chopped, makes about the same quantity as a medium garlic clove.

To get more juice out of a lemon, drop it in boiling water for a minute, or at least roll it back and forth on the kitchen counter. Rub lemon on raw mushrooms to keep them white.

When using bread to make toast cups, toast the unused sections in a slow oven and whirl in a blender or food processor to make your own bread crumbs.

When flouring food, unless the recipe specifies otherwise, do it just before putting the food in the pan; otherwise you will have a gummy rather than a crisp exterior. However, if you are flouring and then dipping in egg and then in bread crumbs to make a crust, do this an hour or two in advance and refrigerate to give the coating a chance to adhere.

When arranging a platter of appetizers with a dip in the center, use green florist's tape to fasten the bowl to the plate, thus avoiding spills when the platter is passed.

In the presentation of food, the eye receives the first impression and influences the taste sensation to follow. Hence, when you are arranging food, consider adding colors and garnishes, but make these edible. A bunch of parsley or watercress with a few cherry tomatoes or shiny olives will perk up a plate. If you have the time, a tomato rose, radish flower, or scallion brush will add a festive touch.

Note on serving olives: if you provide pitted or stuffed ones, the ashtrays will need emptying far less often.

For a large gathering, prepare two or three platters of the same item and keep the extras in the refrigerator as replacements when a dish begins to look messy.

My friends have often teased me because before any party, even one for only six people, I make out the menu and draw up a battle plan of what has to be purchased and the order of preparation. Then I do a dry run with the plates I expect to use on the buffet table and draw a map of the table. On the menu, I list next to each item the plate it is to be served in and all necessary serving dishes and implements. The day before I make a final timetable of what has to be done and exactly when, so that no matter how involved I am with my guests, I will not burn something. This is also useful when you have someone in the kitchen to help serve. In addition, I carry a parking-meter timer in my pocket, so I can hear its ring wherever I am.

This may sound complex, but I can be a more relaxed hostess if I don't have to worry about whether I remembered to heat the main dish or remove the mousse from the freezer. I proved the theory when my husband and I celebrated our one-hundredth birthday (our combined ages, that is) with a cocktail-buffet dinner for ninety-two people, all the cooking done by me. I spent the afternoon before the party having my hair done and taking a sun bath in the comforting consciousness of 900 cookies in the freezer, and a twenty-two-piece antipasto and a full meal ready to go.

Dips, Spreads, and Sauces

Dips
and Spreads

The ubiquitous onion-soup dip and clam dip have obscured the fact that dips and spreads can be the stars rather than the road company stand-ins of a cocktail table. They existed in foreign cuisines long before the advent of the American cocktail party. Among these are the Russian eggplant dish often called "poor man's caviar," the Middle Eastern *baba ghanouj* (also an eggplant-based spread) and *hummus bi tahini* (a chick-pea spread), Mexican guacamole, and Hungarian Liptauer cheese dip, all included here.

I have given relatively few dips; most of these recipes are for thicker spreads. (This is partly for the sake of my own carpets and my guests' clothes.) For serious dieters some low-calorie dips are included.

With a dip or spread, do not limit yourself to some sort of a chip as a carrier. Supermarkets now stock all types of foreign breads; try the Middle Eastern pita bread or the Scandinavian flatbreads or some of the imported crisp crackers. Bread sticks or English Twiglets also are excellent with most spreads. And chilled raw vegetables (*crudités*) marry well with almost any spread or dip.

Additional spreads and dips appear elsewhere in the book; see index.

HUNGARIAN LIPTAUER DIPPING SAUCE

¼ cup cottage cheese
¼ cup sour cream
1½ teaspoons caraway seeds
1 teaspoon grated onion
1 teaspoon prepared mustard (German or Dijon)
1 teaspoon capers, drained and chopped
1 teaspoon Hungarian sweet paprika
¼ teaspoon anchovy paste
1 teaspoon chopped chives

Beat the cottage cheese and sour cream with a wire whisk until smooth. Add remaining ingredients. Chill. Serve with raw vegetables. *Makes about ½ cup.*

YOGURT SKINNY DIP

½ cup drained yogurt
2 tablespoons chopped fresh parsley
2 tablespoons chopped dill
2 tablespoons chopped chives
1 teaspoon finely minced onion
3 dashes cayenne pepper
¼ teaspoon salt

Combine all ingredients and chill. Serve with raw vegetables. *Makes about 1 cup.*

Drained Yogurt

Yogurt, when drained, is similar in texture to sour cream and a great deal less fattening.

Put the yogurt in a strainer over a bowl and refrigerate several hours or overnight. Undrained yogurt can be substituted if desired in any recipe calling for drained yogurt. *1 cup yogurt makes ½ cup drained.*

CUKE-YOGURT DIP

To ½ cup drained yogurt, add 1 cucumber, peeled, seeded, and finely grated, 3 tablespoons minced scallions, 3 tablespoons finely chopped fresh dill, 6 grinds pepper, and ¼ teaspoon salt. *Makes about 1 cup.*

CURRY-YOGURT DIP

To ½ cup drained yogurt, add 1½ teaspoons curry powder, ½ clove garlic, crushed, and ¼ teaspoon ground ginger. *Makes about ½ cup.*

PIQUANT YOGURT DIP

6 ounces cream cheese with chives
6 tablespoons drained yogurt
¼ teaspoon chili sauce
1 tablespoon prepared horseradish
2 cloves garlic, put through press (½ teaspoon)
2 tablespoons chopped chives
¼ teaspoon anchovy paste
4 grinds black pepper
2 teaspoons onion juice

Let the cheese come to room temperature. Mash it in a large bowl, add the rest of the ingredients, and mix until all are well blended. Chill. Use as a dip for raw vegetables or seafood. *Makes about 1 cup.*

MOCK SOUR CREAM

1 12-ounce container low-fat cottage cheese

Cream in a blender or food processor until smooth. *Makes 1¼ cups.*

DIETERS' DILL DIP

1 cup blended cottage cheese
6 tablespoons chopped fresh dill
½ teaspoon finely chopped shallots
2 dashes Worchestershire sauce
½ clove garlic, finely chopped (¼ teaspoon)

Combine, cover, and chill. *Makes about 1 cup.*

GREEN DIP
To 1 cup blended cottage cheese, add 6 tablespoons minced celery leaves and 3 tablespoons finely minced scallions. *Makes about 1 cup.*

SWISS DIP
To 1 cup blended cottage cheese, add 6 tablespoons grated Sap Sago cheese. Sprinkle with paprika before serving. *Makes about 1½ cups.*

GUACAMOLE

Because this has become common at cocktail parties, no book of hors d'oeuvres can omit it. Properly made, it is a smooth refreshing treat whether served with corn chips or chicharrones (fried pork rinds, available in bags in supermarkets), or with raw vegetables. Leftovers make a delicious dressing for a spinach salad. There are many variations, but two ingredients are constant: a ripe avocado and citrus juice (the acid helps to prevent the avocado from darkening). Buy avocados in advance; those found in the market are usually as hard as cannonballs and require some ripening. If an avocado ripens before you are ready to use it, it can be kept for a few days in the refrigerator.

1 large ripe avocado (about 1½ pounds)
2 tablespoons seeded, finely chopped, green chili peppers
¼ cup finely chopped onion

¾ teaspoon salt
1 clove garlic, minced (½ teaspoon)
3 tablespoons peeled, seeded, chopped tomatoes
2 tablespoons lemon or lime juice
½ teaspoon chopped fresh coriander (optional)

If possible, make this the day you plan to serve it, although I have held it overnight with no adverse effects. Halve the avocado lengthwise, remove the pit, and scoop out the flesh with a large spoon into a mixing bowl. Reserve the pit. With a fork, coarsely mash the avocado flesh. Split the chilies and rinse under cold running water to remove the seeds; then chop fine and add, along with the chopped onion, salt, garlic, tomatoes, and lemon juice. Mix well, put into a small dish, bury the pit in the center, and cover tightly. Refrigerate. When ready to serve, remove the pit, stir the mixture again, and transfer it to a serving dish. If you can obtain fresh coriander (cilantro) in a Chinese or Latin American market, sprinkle about ½ teaspoon on top. *Makes about 1 cup.*

(I have yet to receive an adequate scientific explanation for the fact that the pit keeps the avocado flesh from darkening, but it sure works.)

YULE DIP

4 ounces cream cheese
2 tablespoons chopped cucumber (peeled and seeded)
2 tablespoons chopped radishes
2 teaspoons chopped scallions
2 tablespoons chopped red or green pepper
2 tablespoons chopped dill
2 tablespoons Salad Seasoning
4 tablespoons sour cream

GARNISH
chopped parsley
sliced radishes

Soften the cheese to room temperature. Add the rest of the ingredients except the garnish and mix well. Chill. Put in a bowl and decorate with a ring of chopped parsley and radish slices. Serve with raw vegetables, crackers, or cocktail rye or pumpernickel. *Makes about 1¼ cups.*

CHILI-CHEESE DIP
(Chili con Queso)

This hot dip, which originated in northern Mexico, is a perfect prelude to an outdoor barbecue and just as welcome on a gusty winter night. You can increase its potency by adding more chilies. To seed the chilies, split them and rinse under cold running water; dry thoroughly on paper towels.

    2 tablespoons butter
    1 cup finely chopped onions
    2 cloves garlic, finely chopped (1 teaspoon)
    1 28-ounce can tomatoes, well drained and chopped
    2 4-ounce cans roasted and peeled green chili peppers,
       rinsed, seeded, and chopped
    2 teaspoons salt
    8 dashes Tabasco
    1½ pounds Monterey Jack cheese or sharp Cheddar, grated

In the top of a double boiler, melt the butter and sauté the onion and garlic until translucent. Place the pan in its bottom over almost boiling water. Add the tomatoes, chilies, salt, Tabasco, and grated cheese. Stir and cook over simmering water for about ½ hour or until the mixture has thickened. Serve in a chafing dish with *tostados* (heated tortillas), corn chips, or raw vegetables. This keeps in the refrigerator for several days and is delicious spooned over vegetables or hamburgers. To reheat, place in double boiler top, over hot water, until hot, stirring occasionally. *Makes 4 cups.*

Can be frozen. Defrost overnight in the refrigerator and heat as above.

ORANGE-SOY DIP

⅓ cup orange marmalade
1 teaspoon grated orange rind
¼ cup lemon juice
¼ cup soy sauce
1 clove garlic, finely chopped (½ teaspoon)
1 teaspoon grated fresh ginger
1 teaspoon cornstarch
1 tablespoon cold water

Combine the marmalade, orange rind, lemon juice, soy sauce, garlic, and ginger. Bring to a boil. Dissolve the cornstarch in the cold water and add it to the hot sauce, stirring constantly until sauce thickens. Serve hot. *Makes ¾ cup.*

ITALIAN CHICK-PEA SPREAD

2 cups canned chick-peas, washed and drained
    (1 20-ounce can)
2 tablespoons tarragon wine vinegar
⅔ cup olive oil
¼ cup finely chopped scallions
2 cloves garlic, minced (1 teaspoon)
1 teaspoon salt
½ teaspoon freshly ground black pepper

GARNISH
1 tablespoon chopped chives, chopped parsley,
    or chopped ripe olives

Place the chick-peas in strainer and run cold water over them. Drain well. In a bowl, with a wire whisk, beat together vinegar and olive oil. Stir in the rest of the ingredients and mix well. Pour over chick-peas and stir to coat them. Cover and refrigerate overnight. Place approximately one-third of the mixture at a time in an electric blender. Blend, stopping occasionally to scrape the sides. When the various ingredients are blended, place in a bowl and continue with the rest of the mixture the same way. (If you use a food processor, you can process all the ingredients at the same time.) Refrigerate, covered, for a few hours or overnight. Before serving, sprinkle with chopped parsley or chopped ripe olives, and serve with bread sticks or celery stalks. *Makes about 2½ cups.*

EMERALD SPREAD

> 6 ounces cream cheese with chives
> 1 bunch watercress
> 3 tablespoons chopped chives
> 1 tablespoon onion juice
> 2 tablespoons sour cream or yogurt

Let the cheese come to room temperature in a bowl. Trim off the tough stems of the watercress and discard; wash the leaves thoroughly and dry. Place on a board and chop fine with a large chef's knife. (This should yield ⅔ cup.) Add the watercress, chopped chives, onion juice, and sour cream or yogurt to the softened cheese. With a large spoon, mix until well blended. Chill for a few hours or overnight.

Serve with raw vegetables or crackers. *Makes about 1¼ cups.*

ITALIAN GREEN SPREAD

This derives most of its bite from the pungent Italian salad green arugula (also called rocket). I first encountered this in Rome years ago, but at home I searched for it in vain, even in many Italian markets. Now, although not yet a supermarket staple, in season it can be purchased in most produce stores. Used with other, blander ingredients it perks up not only the flavor but also the color of the dish. If you have an herb garden or a vegetable plot, try to find room for it; it is among the easiest of the lettuce family to grow.

> 1 3-ounce package cream cheese with chives
> 1 bunch arugula (rocket)

3 ounces Italian salami, ground fine
2 tablespoons chopped Italian red onion
3 grinds black pepper

Let the cheese come to room temperature to soften. Trim the ends from the arugula, wash it thoroughly, spin-dry, and roll in a clean towel. Place the leaves on a chopping board and chop fine with a large knife. You should have 1 cup of leaves. Put the salami through the fine blade of a food grinder or chop in a food processor. Combine all the ingredients, mix well, and chill, covered. Serve with melba toast, large bread sticks, or raw vegetables. *Makes 1 cup.*

VARIATION
Omit the salami and black pepper. Add the chopped arugula, ½ clove garlic, crushed (¼ teaspoon), ¼ cup chopped red onion, and 1 teaspoon anchovy paste to the softened cheese.

EGGPLANT WITH SESAME PASTE
(Baba Ghanouj)

Both this purée and Sesame Chick-Pea Spread (see index) have long been popular in the Middle East and are rapidly becoming cocktail-party favorites in this country. Sesame paste (*tahini*) is available in specialty food shops and many health food stores. Note that when you open the can or jar you will probably find that the paste has separated. Stir it vigorously with a spoon and then pour it into an electric blender and run at high speed till mixture is reconstituted.

1 eggplant (about 1 pound)
2 cloves garlic
1 teaspoon salt
¼ cup sesame paste (*tahini*)
¼ cup lemon juice
¼ teaspoon freshly ground black pepper
½ cup pine nuts, toasted
¼ cup finely chopped parsley

Preheat oven to 400°. Line a pie plate with foil. Prick the skin of the eggplant in a few places and place on foil. Bake for about 40 minutes or until the eggplant collapses. When it is cool enough to handle, peel off the skin and break up the pulp. Put the shredded pulp in a bowl of an electric blender or a food processor and purée for 2 minutes. Crush the garlic in the salt. Add to the eggplant with the *tahini*, lemon juice, and pepper. Blend until all the ingredients are incorporated. Place in a bowl, cover, and chill for a few hours or a day. Serve garnished with the toasted pine nuts and chopped parsley. Surround the serving bowl with sesame crackers or heated pita bread. *Makes about 2 cups.*

Note. To toast pine nuts, place them on a baking sheet in a preheated 350° oven for about 8 minutes. Watch closely after 5 minutes, as they burn very quickly.

FLIP'S VEGETARIAN RUSSIAN DELIGHT

This is my sister's version of the tangy eggplant mixture often called "poor man's caviar." After many futile efforts to ascertain the origin of that name, I can only agree with Elizabeth David that it is "idiotic." By any name, however, it is a refreshing and unusual spread.

  1 eggplant (1 pound)
  2 large tomatoes, peeled, seeded, and chopped
    into ¼-inch dice
  ½ cup chopped onion
  3 cloves garlic, finely minced (1½ teaspoons)
  1 teaspoon sugar
  1 teaspoon salt
  ½ teaspoon freshly ground black pepper
  2 tablespoons red wine vinegar
  2 tablespoons olive oil
  1 teaspoon sesame oil
  ¼ cup finely chopped parsley

Preheat oven to 400°. Place the unpeeled eggplant on an oven-proof pan and bake for 20 minutes. Turn and bake for 20 minutes more. Using a potholder to protect your fingers, gently press the eggplant; it should be slightly soft all over. When it is done, remove it from the oven and split it open to prevent a steamy flavor from developing. As soon as the eggplant is cool enough to handle, remove the skin, leaving the pulp as nearly intact as possible. With a sharp knife, chop the eggplant meat into ¼-inch dice. Do not mash it; it should resemble large grains of caviar, not mashed potatoes. Put the chopped eggplant into a bowl. Add the tomatoes, onion, garlic, sugar, salt, pepper, vinegar, and olive oil. Mix thoroughly and taste for seasoning. (Remember that chilled dishes need more salt.) Chill for at least 3 hours. Remove from the refrigerator long enough before serving for the eggplant to reach room temperature. Just before serving, stir in the sesame oil and sprinkle the parsley on top. Serve with sesame crackers or heated pita bread. This will keep for a week in the refrigerator, but you may want to drain off the liquid that accumulates after a few days. *Makes about 4 cups.*

CAPE COD EGGPLANT SPREAD

1 medium eggplant (about 8½ inches long)
1 7½-ounce can minced clams, drained
¼ cup chopped parsley
3 tablespoons clam juice
2 cloves garlic, chopped (1 teaspoon)
1½ teaspoons salt
½ teaspoon freshly ground black pepper
2 tablespoons chopped pimiento

Preheat oven to 400°. Place the whole eggplant on a foil-lined baking sheet. Bake about 40 minutes or until the skin seems to have collapsed. Cool the eggplant until it can be handled, then peel and chop it. Place the chopped eggplant in a strainer over a bowl and let it drain for ½ hour. After it has drained there should be 1½ cups eggplant. Add the rest of the ingredients and mix well. Chill. Serve with dark bread or heated pita bread. *Makes 1½ cups.*

MUSHROOM SPREAD

> 1 3-ounce package cream cheese with chives
> about ¼ pound fresh mushrooms, caps only
> 1 teaspoon onion juice
> ½ teaspoon salt
> ⅛ teaspoon white pepper

Put the cheese in a bowl and let come to room temperature. Wipe the mushroom caps with a damp paper towel and chop fine. Add mushrooms, onion juice, salt, and pepper to the softened cream cheese. Chill, covered. Do not make this more than 6 hours in advance, or the mushrooms will give off too much liquid and also darken. Serve with raw vegetables or whole-wheat crackers. Or spread on slices of grisson (Swiss air-dried beef similar to prosciutto), roll into cylinders, chill, and cut into slices. *Makes about ¾ cup.*

PINK VEGETABLE SPREAD

> 3 ounces cream cheese
> 3 ounces Danish Tilsit cheese
> ¼ teaspoon Hungarian sweet paprika
> ¼ teaspoon German mustard
> 1 tablespoon finely chopped chives
> 2 tablespoons finely chopped red sweet pepper
> 2 tablespoons finely chopped green sweet pepper
> ¼ cup finely chopped scallions
> 1 teaspoon caraway seeds
> ¼ teaspoon onion juice
> ¼ teaspoon celery seed
> 1 teaspoon finely chopped dill
> 3 tablespoons sour cream

Let the cheeses soften to room temperature. Beat until combined. Add the rest of the ingredients and stir until they are well distributed. Cover and chill for a few hours or overnight. Serve with thin squares of pumpernickel bread or with raw vegetables. *Makes about 1½ cups.*

HONG KONG SPREAD

¼ cup sesame seeds
1 tablespoon, plus 1 teaspoon, soy sauce
½ teaspoon powdered ginger
6 ounces cream cheese softened to room temperature

Place the sesame seeds on a baking sheet and place in a preheated 300° oven for 10 minutes, stirring occasionally. Let cool on paper towels.

Add the toasted sesame seeds, the soy sauce, and the ginger to the softened cheese. Combine well. Chill, covered. Serve surrounded by sesame-seed crackers. *Makes ⅔ cup.*

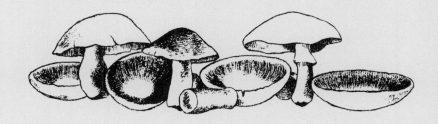

Sauces

Included here are a variety of basic sauces; other sauces appear elsewhere in the book (see index). Since many have a mayonnaise base or contain mayonnaise, it is important to note that I mean homemade mayonnaise. This sleek daffodil-colored sauce is light-years away from the commercial product, and with either an electric blender or a food processor, its making is no longer a tedious chore. Mayonnaise made by either method can be used in any recipe in which mayonnaise is specified.

ELECTRIC-BLENDER MAYONNAISE

    1 egg
    1 teaspoon salt
    ½ teaspoon dry mustard
    ¼ teaspoon white pepper
    2 tablespoons lemon juice
    1 cup vegetable oil, at least half olive oil

Have all ingredients at room temperature. Put the egg, salt, mustard, white pepper, lemon juice, and ¼ cup of the oil in the container. Cover and blend for 1 minute, then remove the feeder cap and pour in the remaining ¾ cup oil in a thin steady stream. If necessary, stop the motor in order to scrape down the sides. When all the oil has been incorporated, taste for seasoning and add if needed. Store in a covered jar in the refrigerator. This will keep

16

for a week, but before using it, take it out of the refrigerator and let it sit a few minutes; then stir and use. *Makes 1 cup.*

LEMON MAYONNAISE
To ⅔ cup mayonnaise add 2 teaspoons grated lemon rind and 4 teaspoons lemon juice.

LEMON-DILL MAYONNAISE
To ½ cup Lemon Mayonnaise add 3 tablespoons finely chopped fresh dill.

ANCHOVY MAYONNAISE
Combine 12 anchovies, mashed (9 teaspoons), 6 tablespoons mayonnaise, and 1 teaspoon dried tarragon.

HORSERADISH MAYONNAISE
Combine 6 tablespoons mayonnaise, 1½ teaspoons prepared horseradish, and 2 tablespoons finely chopped parsley.

ROSY MAYONNAISE
Combine 6 tablespoons mayonnaise, 1½ teaspoons tomato paste, and 12 dashes Worcestershire sauce.

CURRY MAYONNAISE
Combine 6 tablespoons mayonnaise, ½ clove garlic, crushed, 1¼ teaspoons curry powder, and ¼ teaspoon celery salt.

MUSTARD MAYONNAISE
Combine 6 tablespoons mayonnaise and 1½ teaspoons Dijon mustard.

FOOD-PROCESSOR MAYONNAISE

The numerous books recently published relating to the food processor all include instructions for mayonnaise, each with variations in the method and in the amounts of the ingredients. After much experimentation (and many disasters), I finally distilled the following formula, which I find most foolproof and also most truly akin to the product that could previously be achieved only with tedious whisking by hand. Again all ingredients should be at room temperature. This recipe can be used for all variations under Blender Mayonnaise.

1 whole egg
2 egg yolks
1½ teaspoons salt
1½ teaspoons dry mustard
2 cups vegetable oil, at least half olive oil
4 tablespoons (¼ cup) lemon juice
¼ teaspoon white pepper

Use either the plastic or the metal blade of the processor; I prefer the metal one for this. Into the bowl put the egg, egg yolks, salt, and mustard; run the machine for about 1 minute. Have the oil in a small pitcher or Pyrex measuring cup. Pour into the feeding spout in a thin, steady stream. After about half the oil has been added, stop the machine and pour in 2 tablespoons of the lemon juice. Turn on the motor again, and after about 30 seconds resume dribbling in the oil, but at a slightly faster rate. When all the oil has been incorporated, add the rest of the lemon juice and the pepper. Run for another 30 seconds. Taste for seasoning and adjust if necessary. *Makes 2 cups.*

CRABMEAT SAUCE

1 cup fresh crabmeat (about ½ pound) or
  1 7½-ounce can crabmeat
1 teaspoon dried tarragon
2 tablespoons dry vermouth
2 tablespoons lemon juice
2 dashes Tabasco
4 shallots, minced (2 teaspoons)
¼ teaspoon Creole Mustard *

*Creole Mustard can be obtained from Zatarain's, Inc., New Orleans, Louisiana 70114.

1 teaspoon Worcestershire sauce
¼ cup mayonnaise
2 tablespoons sour cream
2 tablespoons chopped chives
1 tablespoon chopped parsley

If you use canned crabmeat, put it into a strainer and rinse under cold water. Drain and dry on paper towels. Remove any tendons. Soak the tarragon in the vermouth and lemon juice in a medium-sized bowl for 5 minutes. Add the crabmeat and shred with a fork. Stir in the Tabasco, cover, and refrigerate for 1 hour. Drain off the liquid, add the remaining ingredients, and mix well. This may be used to coat hard-cooked eggs (see index); decorate each with a slice of pimiento-stuffed olive. *Makes 1 cup.*

DUCK SAUCE, HOMEMADE

Traditionally an accompaniment for roast pork or spareribs, this can also accompany Fried Eggplant and Spring Rolls (see index).

½ cup orange marmalade
½ cup apricot preserves
1 tablespoon soy sauce
1 tablespoon chili sauce
1 tablespoon grated orange rind
2 teaspoons grated lemon rind

Put all the ingredients into the container of an electric blender or the bowl of a food processor and purée until smooth. *Makes about 1 cup.*

GREEN GODDESS DRESSING

Almost every cook has her own favorite version of this San Francisco original. It is extremely versatile—a perfect dip for vegetables, a dressing for salad greens, or a sauce for hot or cold seafood.

2 cloves garlic, peeled and cut in half
2 tablespoons anchovy paste
2 tablespoons chopped chives
6 tablespoons coarsely chopped scallions
1 tablespoon lemon juice
1 tablespoon tarragon wine vinegar
½ cup parsley
½ cup sour cream
1 cup mayonnaise
½ teaspoon salt
pinch freshly ground black pepper
½ teaspoon dried tarragon

Put all the ingredients in the container of an electric blender or the bowl of a food processor and purée until smooth. *Makes about 1 pint.*

HORSERADISH SAUCE

An excellent accompaniment for all types of smoked fish, this also enhances poached fish.

1 cup sour cream
2 teaspoons grated onion
½ teaspoon prepared horseradish
¾ teaspoon Dijon mustard
¼ teaspoon salt
½ cup finely chopped fresh dill

Combine all the ingredients and chill. *Makes about 1 cup.*

PEKING DIPPING SAUCE

A good accompaniment for egg rolls, spring rolls, or Chinese dumplings, as well as for beer-battered seafood or chilled shellfish. This has been a standby of our household for years and keeps for weeks in the refrigerator.

6 tablespoons minced scallions
2 ¼-inch slices fresh ginger, minced (1 teaspoon)
2 cloves garlic, minced
2 teaspoons sugar
¼ cup water
¼ cup light soy sauce
4 teaspoons malt vinegar

Combine all ingredients in a jar and shake to mix. *Makes ⅔ cup.*

PESTO SAUCE

With the introduction of the electric blender, this beautiful green sauce, which originated in Genoa, gained well-deserved popularity over here. Few people had been willing to make it in the traditional way by mincing the ingredients and puréeing them with a mortar and pestle, but the blender makes it easy to produce a most acceptable facsimile. Fresh basil, the essential ingredient, was formerly available only in summer, but now the sauce can be frozen and used the year around. Pesto is used primarily for pasta as a delightful change from the more usual tomato sauce, but it also can enliven raw tomatoes or lightly sautéed zucchini.

2 cups basil leaves, tightly packed
3 cloves garlic, peeled and halved
½ cup pine nuts
½ teaspoon salt
½ cup olive oil
½ cup freshly grated Parmesan cheese

Place all the ingredients in the container of an electric blender or the bowl of a food processor and mix until a smooth paste has formed. Stop the motor occasionally and scrape the sides with a rubber spatula. Put into a jar or freezer container and float about ½ inch of olive oil on top. This will keep for weeks in the refrigerator or months in the freezer. To use, scrape off the layer of oil. *Makes about 1½ cups.*

PESTO MAYONNAISE

Combine ¾ cup mayonnaise with ¼ cup plus 2 teaspoons Pesto Sauce. This may be used to coat hard-cooked eggs (see index); decorate the coated eggs with thin strips of pimiento. *Makes 1 cup.*

RED CAVIAR SAUCE

When I first made this, it was considered a delicious inexpensive dip for vegetables or chips, but the cost of red caviar has now elevated it to company status. Most versions of this combine the caviar with sour cream, but I prefer cream cheese as the base, since the caviar eggs tend to break up a bit in the mixing and provide enough liquid.

8 ounces cream cheese with chives, softened
    to room temperature
2 tablespoons chopped scallions
2 tablespoons chopped chives
1 4-ounce jar salmon roe caviar (do not use lumpfish)

Put the cream cheese in a small bowl, add the scallions and 2 tablespoons chives and blend well. Fold in the caviar. This may be used to coat hard-cooked eggs (see index); sprinkle coated eggs with additional chopped chives. *Makes 1 cup.*

REMOULADE SAUCE

½ cup mayonnaise
2 tablespoons chopped shallots
2 cloves garlic, finely minced
2 teaspoons capers, drained and chopped
2 teaspoons chopped parsley
2 tablespoons fresh tarragon, finely chopped,
    or 1 teaspoon dried

⅛ teaspoon anchovy paste
1½ teaspoons Creole Mustard *
dash Tabasco
⅛ teaspoon salt

Combine all ingredients and chill. *Makes about ½ cup.*

TARTARE SAUCE

1 cup mayonnaise
2 tablespoons lemon juice
2 tablespoons finely chopped gherkins
1 teaspoon finely chopped capers
1 teaspoon minced shallots
1 tablespoon minced scallions
2 tablespoons finely chopped parsley
1 teaspoon chopped chives
dash Tabasco
1 teaspoon Dijon mustard

Mix all ingredients thoroughly. Refrigerate for a few hours. *Makes about 1½ cups.*

VELVETY COCKTAIL SAUCE

¼ cup mayonnaise
¼ cup sour cream
¼ cup chili sauce
¼ cup Escoffier Sauce Robert
2 tablespoons Escoffier Sauce Diable
2 tablespoons port wine
2 tablespoons finely chopped parsley
2 teaspoons dried tarragon

*Creole Mustard can be obtained from Zatarain's, Inc., New Orleans, Louisiana 70114.

Mix all ingredients thoroughly. Refrigerate for a few hours. *Makes about 1¼ cups.*

VINAIGRETTE SAUCE

> 4 cloves garlic, crushed (2 teaspoons)
> ½ cup olive oil
> 2 tablespoons lemon juice
> ½ teaspoon Dijon mustard
> ½ teaspoon salt
> ¼ teaspoon freshly ground black pepper

In a medium-sized jar, soak the garlic in the oil overnight at room temperature, covered. Strain out the garlic and return the oil to the jar. (There will be about 6 tablespoons of garlic-flavored oil remaining.) Add the remaining ingredients. Put the lid on the jar and shake vigorously until all the ingredients are thoroughly homogenized. Store in the refrigerator. Bring to room temperature before using. Serve over cold beef, seafood, or vegetables. *Makes a generous ½ cup.*

SAUCES FOR HARD-COOKED EGGS

Although a bit more awkward as a cocktail accompaniment than deviled eggs, hard-cooked eggs coated with a tempting sauce make an attractive addition to an hors d'oeuvre table or an antipasto or the French *hors d'oeuvre varié.* If you wish to do without plates and forks, have melba toast or small slices of French bread nearby to be used as carriers. The amounts given for the following sauces will cover 6 hard-cooked eggs. Cut eggs in half lengthwise, place them on a shallow platter, and cover generously with sauce. (Other sauces that can be used to coat eggs are Crabmeat Sauce, Pesto Mayonnaise, and Red Caviar Sauce; see index.)

Anchovy Sauce

6 tablespoons sour cream
6 tablespoons mayonnaise
4½ teaspoons anchovy paste
2 tablespoons minced onion
1 tablespoon lemon juice
1 tablespoon finely minced parsley, plus additional parsley

Combine all the ingredients. Decorate the coated eggs with additional parsley. *Makes 1 cup.*

Calorie Counters Herb Sauce

1 cup drained yogurt (see index)
10 tablespoons finely chopped watercress
6 tablespoons finely chopped parsley
1 tablespoon fresh tarragon or 1 teaspoon dried
2 teaspoons finely chopped chives
2 cloves garlic, minced (1 teaspoon)
½ teaspoon salt
¼ teaspoon freshly ground black pepper

Combine all the ingredients and purée in an electric blender or a food processor. This should not be made more than 24 hours in advance, or the herbs will lose their bright green color. *Makes 1 cup.*

Indian Sauce

1 cup mayonnaise
5 teaspoons finely chopped chutney
2 teaspoons curry powder

Combine all ingredients. *Makes 1 generous cup.*

Cold
Hors d'Oeuvres

For either a small dinner party or a gigantic cocktail bash, cold hors d'oeuvres are the safest bet for any hostess. Nearly all of them can be prepared in advance, need no pot-watching or tending after they are served, and being mostly help-yourself items, reduce the need for service.

Do remember that in most cases "cold" means only slightly chilled; ice-cold food has very little flavor. In preparing anything to be served chilled, use more salt and more seasoning in general than for hot food. If you are serving a large group, have extra platters ready in the refrigerator to replace dishes on the serving table.

Though cold hors d'oeuvres are simple, they need not be clichés; the following pages give some idea of the range at your disposal.

Cold
Vegetables

Cold vegetables, either raw, or cooked and then chilled, have long been important in most foreign cuisines, but only recently have Americans begun to appreciate the clean, crunchy taste of raw vegetables and to recognize their usefulness as dippers in place of the potato chip and its relatives.

Most cold vegetables can be prepared in advance and require very little last-minute attention. They are usually light and are low in calories, especially if served with a yogurt-based dip. The Mediterranean countries, although they specialize in serving stuffed vegetables hot, have also devised many savory combinations that are equally delicious served at room temperature. Whether vegetables are to be served hot or cold, remember to cook them *al dente* —that is, until barely tender. By that method they retain more vitamins and their individual flavors are still evident. Many canned vegetables can also be the basis of tasty treats.

CHILLED RAW VEGETABLES
(Crudités)

A platter of decoratively arranged raw vegetables set on crushed ice is one item I almost always include on an hors d'oeuvre table. These are light but satisfying, and do not ruin the appetite for a meal to follow. Dieters delight in them; they can ignore the dips and eat the raw vegetables *au naturel* or sprinkled with kosher salt or seasoned salt. So many dips are compatible with them that one can serve them often without repeating the same theme. If you have the time and patience, you can carve all sorts of flower shapes. Red radish roses, white radish lilies, tomato or turnip roses, and scallion brushes interspersed with cauliflower and broccoli buds, cherry tomatoes, celery and carrot sticks, embedded with toothpicks in a foil-covered cabbage and set in a straw basket make an edible centerpiece that will impress any guest. It does have one drawback, however—no one wants to start picking the masterpiece apart.

The choice of vegetables to serve need only be limited by the season. Cucumber sticks, red pepper and green pepper strips, and raw mushrooms, are obvious additions; other choices are peeled finger avocados (seedless), thin-sliced black radishes, fennel, kirbys (pickling cucumbers). Many young vegetables are as tasty raw as cooked, if not tastier; try young, slender asparagus, peeled broccoli spears, young green beans, rounds of peeled kohlrabi or jicama, whole snow peas, strips of zucchini and of peeled white turnips. Shelled fava beans are delicious dipped in kosher salt. Even the more unusual of these can be obtained in season from a good produce market.

I usually serve this "rabbit food" with a choice of two dips, or even three at a large cocktail party. If you are having more than twenty guests, set up two platters each of vegetables and dips and place them in different parts of the room. Also prepare a supply of replacements to be kept chilled in the refrigerator. After about an hour, you will probably need to check the platters, pour off the accumulated water, replace the ice, and replenish the vegetables.

QUICK ANTIPASTO

Everyone enjoys an antipasto—perhaps because the variety of components guarantees something for everyone. An antipasto can easily be assembled with on-hand ingredients, though it can be made more luxurious by items from an Italian delicatessen or the appetizer department of a supermarket.

Line a platter with lettuce and add as many of the following as you wish.

artichoke hearts
cannellini beans
pickled eggplant
caponata
marinated mushrooms
fried and stuffed peppers
olives and olive salad
picked vegetables (*giardiniera*)
anchovies
tuna fish
sardines
(The preceding are available in jars or cans)

hard-cooked eggs
salami
pepperoni
prosciutto
mortadella
capicolla
Gorgonzola and provolone cheeses
cherry tomatoes or tomato slices
celery
carrot sticks
radishes
scallions

Provide olive oil and red wine vinegar in cruets, and have Italian bread and Italian bread sticks (*grissini*) in baskets nearby. Be sure to provide small plates and plenty of paper napkins.

MAURICE MOORE-BETTY'S VEGETABLE ANTIPASTO

This colorful vegetable mélange, with its mild sweet and sour sauce, is a refreshing addition to any appetizer tray. Refrigerated, it will keep a week, so it can be prepared in advance, and any leftovers will make a delicious salad. Do not be put off by the number of ingredients; once they are assembled and prepared, the cooking is a matter of minutes. This recipe incorporates my modifications of the original.

1 stalk celery
¼ pound fresh green beans
2 carrots
¼ pound small white mushrooms
12 small white onions
1 small head cauliflower
2 small green peppers
1 small eggplant, unpeeled
1 cup olive oil
3 cloves garlic, chopped
1 bay leaf
8 large green olives
12 large ripe olives
3 whole preserved red pimientos
1 cup tomato catchup
1 cup Dessaux French red wine vinegar
4 tablespoons sugar
1 tablespoon prepared mustard (Dijon or Coleman's)
salt and pepper to taste (I use 2 teaspoons salt and
    over ¼ teaspoon freshly ground black pepper)

Cut the celery into 1-inch pieces. Break the green beans into small pieces. Scrape the carrots and cut into 1-inch pieces. Wipe the mushrooms with a damp towel and quarter them. (I leave them whole, if they are small.) Cut the onions into quarters (leave small ones whole). Trim the cauliflower and break into small buds. Remove the pith and seeds from the green peppers and cut into thin strips. Cut the eggplant into small cubes. Heat the olive oil in a large, heavy skillet and add the garlic; when it is golden, remove and discard. Add the bay leaf and all the vegetables and cook over medium heat until tender but still crisp. (I find 10 minutes is adequate, but keep turning the vegetables in the skillet.) Pit the olives, cut the pimientos into broad strips, and add both to the vegetables. Stir in the tomato catchup, vinegar, sugar, mustard, and salt and pepper, and cook for another 5 minutes.

Cool and then chill in the refrigerator before serving. The important thing to remember when preparing this dish is that the whole should be *al dente*. *Makes about 20 servings.*

VEGETABLES À LA GRECQUE

Almost any vegetable lends itself to this simple but piquant treatment. The basic approach is to prepare a spicy broth in which each vegetable is poached separately. Cooking each vegetable individually is necessary, not to prevent the mingling of flavors, but because each requires a different cooking time to be *al dente* when finished. Besides the vegetables mentioned in the recipe, one can also use beans, fennel, celery hearts, leeks, cucumbers, cauliflower, or strips of eggplant. Once poached, the vegetables can be kept refrigerated for five days and used alone, in combination, or as part of a salad. When serving them as an hors d'oeuvre, provide small plates and forks.

> 1⅔ cups chicken broth
> ½ cup vermouth
> ¼ cup olive oil
> ⅓ cup lemon juice
> 1 teaspoon salt
> ¼ cup minced shallots
> 6 sprigs parsley
> ¼ cup celery leaves
> ¼ teaspoon fennel seeds
> 6 coriander seeds, lightly crushed
> 8 peppercorns, lightly crushed
> ¼ teaspoon thyme
> small bay leaf
> 2 cloves garlic, split
>
> GARNISH (optional)
> finely chopped parsley and chives

Put all the ingredients into a large saucepan. Bring to a boil, cover, and simmer slowly for 30 minutes. Strain the liquid into a bowl through a fine sieve or a strainer lined with a double thickness of cheesecloth. Using a large spoon, press to extract as much of the liquid as possible. Pour this court bouillon back into the saucepan. Bring it to a boil, add the chosen vegetable, cover the pan, reduce the heat to simmer, and cook the appropriate time (see following list). With a slotted spoon, remove the vegetable to a serving dish, and repeat the procedure for additional vegetables. When all the vegetables are cooked, if more than ½ cup of the poaching liquid remains, rapidly boil it down to ⅓ cup. Pour this over the vegetables and let them cool. Cover them and chill overnight or longer; let them come to room temperature before serving. If you are serving more than one vegetable, arrange them decoratively in contrasting color groups. Sprinkle with finely chopped parsley and chives, if you wish.

Approximate cooking times for a few vegetables follow (make sure they do not overcook).

button mushrooms, stems cut off at base—10 minutes
peppers, red and green, cut into ¾-inch strips—10 minutes
tiny artichokes—about 15 minutes, or until a knife easily
   pierces the base
zucchini, cut into 1-inch widths—15 minutes
asparagus—depends on diameter, test after 5 minutes
Broth for 1 pound of vegetables.

COLD STUFFED VEGETABLES

Many vegetables lend themselves to being stuffed for a cocktail nibble. The preparation of some of the vegetables is time-consuming, but many of the fillings can be frozen and the stuffed vegetables assembled hours in advance, covered tightly with plastic wrap, and refrigerated. Your own refrigerator will inspire other combinations. Besides these general suggestions, specific recipes for stuffed cold vegetables are included in this section.

Canned or fresh artichoke bottoms filled with any fish spread, Red Caviar Dip or homemade or canned pâté. Whole cooked artichokes, choke removed and leaves spread fanlike around the heart, with a dab of Lemon Mayonnaise and a small shrimp or piece of crabmeat on the edible part of each leaf.

Tiny canned beets, centers scooped out with a melon-baller and filled with a herring spread or Roquefort Spread.

Brussels sprouts, cooked just till tender (8 to 10 minutes), centers scooped out and filled with any meat or fish spread.

Celery or endive stalks, cut into 2-inch lengths and filled with Steak Tartare, Chopped Chicken Liver, any fish spread, or cheese spreads such as Roquefort or Gorgonzola or Liptauer.

Cucumber cups or boats filled with smoked salmon spread, any fish spread, or a Gorgonzola spread. Use 2 slender cucumbers about 6 inches long and ¼ cup spread. If the cucumbers are waxed, peel them with a fluting knife. If you grow your own or are able to purchase untreated cucumbers, simply score the skin with the tines of a fork. Cut the cucumbers crosswise into ¾-inch slices. With a small melon-baller, carefully scoop out the seeds, leaving a base about ¼-inch deep. Turn the cups upside down for a few minutes to drain. Fill each with about ¾ teaspoon of desired filling. Cover and chill at least 1 hour. When ready to serve, sprinkle the filling with finely chopped parsley or put a slice of pitted ripe olive on top. These can also be used to circle a fish mold.

Mushrooms. Choose white, firm ones about 1½ inches in diameter. Wipe them with a damp towel and then immerse for a minute in a bowl of lemon juice diluted with cold water. Drain them well and fill. They make perfect containers for almost any kind of filling: seafood, such as crab or Nova Scotia spread or Red Caviar Dip; meat, such as chopped liver, pâté, liverwurst, deviled ham or Steak Tartare; cheese such as Roquefort-brandy or Camembert-Brie or herb cheese. (See also Hot Hors d'Oeuvres.)

Small onions, parboiled and cooled. Scoop out the centers and fill with smoked salmon spread or Steak Tartare.

Cherry tomatoes, by far the most tedious to tackle, but delicious and attractive containers for all manner of stuffings. The easiest way is to make a slit in the side away from the stem and insert a smoked oyster or smoked clam. Use the stem end as the base; the tomatoes stand better. Or cut a thin slice from the side away from the stem, and with a ½-inch melon-baller carefully scoop out the pulp. Salt the inside lightly and turn the tomatoes upside down to drain for 15 minutes. If the filling is stiff enough, put it into a pastry bag and pipe it into the tomatoes. If it is too liquid, use a ¼ teaspoon measuring spoon to fill them. Top with a sprig of parsley or dill or a tiny piece of ripe olive, depending upon what is appropriate to the filling. Guacamole and most fish, meat, or cheese spreads are good choices.

ARTICHOKE HEARTS STUFFED WITH MUSSELS

3 ounces cream cheese, softened to room temperature
2 tablespoons lemon juice
4 tablespoons chopped fresh dill
3 tablespoons minced onion
1 14-ounce can artichoke hearts (20), rinsed and drained
1 9-ounce can mussels (drained weight)
smoked cod caviar paste (available in tubes in specialty
    food departments or stores)

Put the cream cheese in a bowl, and mix in the lemon juice, dill, and onion. Dry the artichoke hearts on paper towels. Drain the mussels and dry on paper towels. Put a mussel in each artichoke heart. Cover the top of each with ¼ teaspoon of the cheese mixture. Squeeze a dab of smoked cod caviar paste on top. Cover and refrigerate; can be assembled 2 days in advance. *Makes 20.*

ITALIAN BLACK AND WHITE BEANS

This is a dish I first sampled in Rome. I was a bit dubious about the mixture of the lowly bean with caviar, but it tasted even more delicious than it looked, and as soon as I reached home I worked out this recipe.

2 20-ounce cans cannellini beans drained and rinsed
½ cup olive oil
¼ cup lemon juice
4 tablespoons red wine vinegar
2 teaspoons salt
¼ teaspoon freshly ground pepper
2 teaspoons oregano
2 teaspoons basil
4 cloves garlic, minced (2 teaspoons)
1 cup finely chopped scallions
2 tablespoons finely chopped Italian parsley,
   plus additional parsley
1 2-ounce jar black lumpfish caviar

Dry the rinsed beans gently but thoroughly and put them into a bowl. Combine the olive oil, lemon juice, vinegar, salt, pepper, oregano, basil, garlic, scallions, and 2 tablespoons chopped parsley. Pour this marinade over the beans and marinate them in the refrigerator for at least 8 hours or up to 36 hours. Remove about 1 hour before you plan to serve, to let the beans come to room temperature. Just before serving, lightly fold the caviar into the beans. Taste for seasoning; the mixture may need more lemon juice or pepper. Sprinkle additional parsley on top. This is particularly attractive served in a red pottery bowl. Melba toast can be used as a carrier or you can provide small plates and forks. *Makes 3 cups.*

MEATY BEAN SALAD

This zesty mixture is a pleasant addition to an antipasto or can be served alone with small slices of Italian bread. (In either case, it requires plates and forks.) I have served it as a summer lunch, accompanied by Italian bread and a mixed green salad.

1¼ cups, plus 2 tablespoons, salad oil
6 tablespoons red wine vinegar
1 tablespoon, plus 2 teaspoons, Italian seasoning

salt and freshly ground pepper
2 20-ounce cans ceci beans, drained, rinsed, and dried
4 celery ribs with leaves, thinly sliced
1 large red onion, diced
⅓ pound baked ham in one piece, diced
½ pound sliced pepperoni, chopped coarsely, plus 8 additional
    slices for garnish (about ¾ pound in all)

Mix the salad oil, vinegar, Italian seasoning, salt, and pepper together as for a salad dressing. (Use ½ teaspoon salt and a few grindings of pepper at first, and add more if necessary.) Put all the other ingredients into a bowl and pour the dressing over. Turn until the dressing permeates all. Taste for salt and pepper and add more if needed. Marinate about 12 hours in the refrigerator. To serve, place in a shallow serving dish. Roll the additional slices of pepperoni to form cornucopias and tuck them around the edges. A tomato rose in the center makes an attractive decoration. *Makes 2 quarts, about 16 servings.*

DILLED BRUSSELS SPROUTS

Many people who disdain this lovely miniature cabbage are won over with one bite of this tangy, herbed version.

¾ pound fresh Brussels sprouts or 1 10-ounce
    package frozen
1 cup vinegar
½ cup water
1 clove garlic, split
1 dried chili pepper
1 tablespoon dried dill weed
1 teaspoon salt

If using fresh Brussels sprouts, remove any yellow or wilted leaves on the outside, cut a small X in the base of each, and soak them for a few minutes in a bowl of cold water. Combine all the ingredients in a medium-sized saucepan. Bring to a boil, lower the heat, and simmer about 10 minutes or until the sprouts are just tender.

If using frozen sprouts, combine all the ingredients in a medium-sized saucepan and bring to a boil, using a fork to separate the sprouts. Cover the pan and simmer for 5 minutes. Don't overcook; the sprouts will continue to cook while cooling.

Pour the sprouts and liquid into a refrigerator jar, cool, seal, and refrigerate. Serve speared on toothpicks. These will keep at least a week in the refrigerator, and leftovers make a delicious addition to a salad. *Makes 6–8 servings as part of an hors d'oeuvre table.*

CAULIFLOWER NIÇOISE

2 heads cauliflower
1¼ cups mayonnaise
¼ cup sour cream
about ½ cup Dijon mustard
¼ cup finely chopped fresh chives
1 2-ounce can flat anchovies
20 oil-cured black olives
10 cherry tomatoes, halved

Break the cauliflower into flowerets, trimming off most of the base. Bring a large pan of water to the boiling point and add the cauliflower. Cover to bring back to a boil, remove cover, and boil 3 minutes. Immediately drain in a colander placed in a bowl of very cold water. Run cold water over the cauliflower until it is quite cool. Drain well. Combine the mayonnaise, sour cream, and mustard. Beat well to blend. Pour the dressing over the cauliflower, gently turning all pieces until covered. Put into a serving dish about 1½ inches deep. Sprinkle with the chives. Drain the anchovies and place them over the cauliflower in a latticework pattern. In the squares, alternately place olives and cherry tomato halves. Cover with plastic wrap and refrigerate for a few hours or overnight. *Makes about 12 servings.*

STUFFED ESCAROLE ERNESTO

One balmy spring evening my husband and I dined gloriously at Ernesto al Cassia, the country branch of a well-known Roman restaurant, where my minimal Italian established sufficient rapport that almost every delicacy ordered by the other patrons was offered to us to sample. One was escarole rolls. Unfortunately, I could only obtain a rather sketchy list of the main components. This recipe, therefore, is my own version.

2 heads escarole
½ pound sweet Italian sausage
½ cup finely chopped onions
3 cloves garlic, finely minced (1½ teaspoons)
¼ teaspoon fennel seeds
½ teaspoon dried oregano
¼ teaspoon dried marjoram
4 or 5 oil-cured black olives, pitted and
    finely chopped (1 tablespoon)
2 tablespoons finely chopped parsley, plus
    additional parsley
½ cup fine dry bread crumbs
2 tablespoons freshly grated Parmesan cheese
1 egg, beaten
¾ cup olive oil
¼ cup lemon juice
1 clove garlic, crushed

Leaf by leaf, carefully wash the escarole (it always seems to be the muddiest of greens). Reserve the smaller inner leaves for salad. You will need at least 40 large leaves; it is safer to cook some extras. Bring a large pot of salted water to a boil, and blanch the leaves, a few at a time, for 1 minute. Carefully remove them with tongs and spread them on paper towels to dry thoroughly.

Meanwhile, remove the sausage meat from its casing and sauté the meat, breaking it up with a fork, until it turns gray. Remove with a slotted spoon to a medium-sized mixing bowl. Pour off all but 1 tablespoon of the fat and add the onions, sautéing over medium heat until translucent. Stir in the garlic and cook for another minute. Add the onions and garlic to the sausage. Stir in the fennel seeds, oregano, marjoram, olives, 2 tablespoons parsley, bread crumbs, cheese, and egg. Mix to combine well.

Carefully spread out 2 escarole leaves, place the narrow end closest to you, and overlap the leaves. Put a heaping teaspoon of the sausage filling at the narrow end and roll over once, turn the edges in on both sides, and continue rolling until you reach the wider end, completely enclosing the filling. Continue, using 2 leaves at a time, until you have filled all the rolls. Pour ½ cup of the olive oil into a deep 10-inch sauté pan. Place the escarole bundles in the pan, seam side down. Mix the remaining ¼ cup oil, the lemon juice, and the crushed garlic and pour over the rolls. Cover the pan, bring to a boil, and lower to simmer. Cook for 20 minutes, checking once to make sure the rolls are not sticking. Let cool to room temperature and serve sprinkled with additional parsley. These can be prepared up to 3 days in advance, cooled, refrigerated, and brought to room temperature before serving. *Makes about 20 rolls.*

MARY'S STUFFED GRAPE LEAVES
(Dolmadakia Mytilene)

While the Greeks do wondrous things in stuffing peppers, tomatoes, eggplant, and zucchini, their most glorious creation is the stuffed grape leaves called *dolmadakia*. These may be stuffed with meat alone or rice alone, but this combination is the version prepared on the island of Mytilene, where my friend Mary's family has its roots.

    1 1-pound jar grape leaves
    ¾ pound ground chuck beef
    ¼ pound ground lamb
    1 cup chopped green part of scallions
    2 tablespoons crushed dried mint or ¼ cup fresh
    6 tablespoons finely chopped fresh dill

2 tablespoons long-grain rice
1 teaspoon salt
½ teaspoon freshly ground black pepper
2 cloves garlic, finely chopped (1 teaspoon)
¼ cup olive oil
½ cup lemon juice
peel of 1 lemon
lemon wedges
tomato rose

Parboil the grape leaves for 5 minutes. Drain them, rinse under cold water, and dry carefully on paper towels, separating them as you dry them. In a mixing bowl, combine the beef, lamb, scallions, mint, dill, rice, salt, pepper, and garlic. Mix thoroughly. Spread out the grape leaves, shiny side down. Cut off the tough stems. There will probably be some variation in the size of the leaves; set aside the smaller ones for lining the pot. Put a heaping teaspoon of the filling on the lower edge of each leaf. Starting at the base, roll once, tuck in the sides, and continue to roll jelly-roll fashion until you reach the tip. Film the bottom of a large heavy pot with the olive oil; cover with some of the reserved small leaves, and put the filled leaves in, placing them seam side down and touching one another. You will probably have at least two layers. When all the leaves are in the pot, sprinkle the lemon juice over them. Cut the lemon peel in large pieces and tuck around the edges of the pot. On top of the leaves, place, bottom side down, a Pyrex pie plate slightly smaller in diameter than the pot. Pour boiling water into the pie plate almost to reach the rim; place a heavy can on the plate to hold it down. Simmer for 30 minutes, shaking the pan carefully from time to time to make sure the leaves are not sticking. Remove the can and simmer another 30 minutes. Cool and then refrigerate. When ready to serve, bring to room temperature and arrange on a platter with lemon wedges between the leaves and a tomato rose in the center. These can also be served hot—either as soon as they are done or reheated. *Makes about 45 stuffed leaves.*

Can be frozen. Freeze in layers in freezer container. Thaw overnight in the refrigerator.

SURPRISE GRAPE LEAVES

Parboil the grape leaves for 5 minutes, drain, rinse under cold water, and dry carefully on paper towels, separating them as you dry. In a large, heavy skillet, heat ¾ cup olive oil and sauté 2 cups finely chopped onions until they are tender but not browned. Add ½ pound ground chuck beef and continue to sauté until the meat loses its color, stirring continuously with a fork to break up the meat. Add 2 teaspoons salt and ½ teaspoon freshly ground black pepper and stir in ¾ cup rice, turning it constantly for about 5 minutes to coat the kernels with the oil. Pour in ½ cup orange juice and ⅔ cup water and stir well. Bring to a boil, cover, and simmer for 15 minutes or until the liquid has been absorbed. Stir in 3 tablespoons grated orange peel, 1 tablespoon cinnamon, and ¼ cup pine nuts. Let the mixture cool. Proceed as in main recipe, but when all the leaves are in the pot, sprinkle an additional ½ cup orange juice and ½ cup water over the leaves. Cut the peel of 1 orange in eighths and tuck the pieces around the edges of the pot. Cook as in main recipe. For serving, arrange the rolls with orange slices between the leaves and a cluster of Greek olives in the center.

MARINATED FRESH MUSHROOMS

Raw mushrooms make a refreshing nibble but when they are steeped in a marinade, their enhanced flavor makes a regal dish.

1 pound firm medium-sized mushrooms
8 cloves garlic, crushed (4 teaspoons)
¾ cup olive oil
6 tablespoons lemon juice
1 teaspoon salt
½ teaspoon freshly ground black pepper
1 teaspoon Dijon mustard
3 tablespoons fresh tarragon, finely chopped,
    or 1 tablespoon dried

Remove the stems of the mushrooms. (You can save the stems and use them for Duxelles, page 216, or for Mushroom Filling, page 212.) Wipe mushrooms with a damp paper towel. In a medium-sized bowl, combine the remaining ingredients. Beat well with a wire whisk. Add the mushrooms and stir to coat them with the marinade. Let stand at room temperature for 3 hours or cover and refrigerate for 1 or 2 days. When ready to serve, bring the mushrooms to room temperature, drain off the marinade, and put a toothpick into each mushroom. Serve on a platter with a cluster of cherry tomatoes and pitted ripe olives in the center. *Makes about 6 servings.*

CRUNCHY STUFFED OLIVES

8 ripe olives (about 1 inch in diameter), pitted
3 scallions, white part only, cut into 8 pieces each
3 ounces cream cheese, softened to room temperature
1 tablespoon chopped chives
¼ teaspoon Worcestershire sauce
¼ teaspoon celery seed
½ clove garlic, put through a press (¼ teaspoon)
pinch white pepper

Drain the olives and dry them on paper towels. Stuff each with a piece of scallion just large enough to fill the hole. Put the cheese into the bowl of an electric mixer or a food processor. Add the chives, Worcestershire sauce, celery seed, garlic, and pepper. Blend until all the ingredients are combined. Put about 1 teaspoon of the cheese mixture into the palm of your hand and flatten it slightly. Put an olive on the cheese and cover it completely, rolling it between your palms to form a ball. As they are finished, place on a plate. Cover with plastic wrap and refrigerate 1 hour. Remove and smooth out the balls so that they are covered smoothly. Refrigerate for another 2 hours. These may be made 2 days in advance. Serve on their own or use to decorate platters. *Makes 8.*

ONION RINGS

This favorite has long been attributed to James Beard, but Irma Rhode, in *Cool Entertaining*, reports: "In the twenties, in a Parisian establishment described by Polly Adler as 'a house that's not a home,' two slices of leftover breakfast brioches, spread with mayonnaise and filled with a slice of onion, were served with the aperitifs to my brother Bill." (In the 1930s, with Irma and Bill Rhode, James Beard launched his first entry into the food field, a catering company called Hors d'Oeuvre, Inc.)

> 6 slices of firm thin-sliced white bread, or 12 ¼-inch-thick
>   slices of challah
> approximately ½ cup mayonnaise
> 12 very thin slices onion
> salt
> approximately ¾ cup very finely chopped parsley

With a 1½-inch cookie cutter, cut 4 rounds from each slice of bread or 2 rounds from each challah slice. Arrange in 12 pairs. Spread each round with mayonnaise. Using either a slicer or a potato peeler, slice the onions. Put 1 slice on each bread round. Salt slightly, then top with the second round, sandwich fashion. When all are assembled, spread mayonnaise on a piece of waxed paper, and on another piece of waxed paper, sprinkle parsley. Take a sandwich between your thumb and forefinger and roll the edges first in the mayonnaise, then in the chopped parsley. If there are any bare spots, dab mayonnaise on them and dip again in parsley. Place on waxed paper on a flat tray or cookie sheet and cover with waxed paper. Chill well. *Makes 12.*

Note: If it's too difficult to get very thin slices of onions perfectly round, part slices will do; use two or more parts. The thinness is important.

HEARTS OF PALM, NOVA SCOTIA STYLE

An unusual combination of textures and flavors.

½ pound Nova Scotia salmon, thinly sliced (about 11 slices)
5½ teaspoons Lemon-Dill Mayonnaise (see index)
1 14-ounce can hearts of palm (or asparagus tips), drained
¼ cup finely chopped fresh dill

Spread each slice of the salmon with about ½ teaspoon of the Lemon-Dill Mayonnaise. Wrap each slice, mayonnaise side in, around 1 stalk heart of palm or asparagus. Cover with plastic wrap and chill for at least 1 hour. When ready to serve, cut each stalk in half, spear each piece with a toothpick, and sprinkle with the chopped dill. *Makes 22.*

HEARTS OF PALM, ITALIAN STYLE
Use prosciutto instead of salmon, spread each slice with Mustard Mayonnaise (see index), and wrap the stalks. Before serving, sprinkle with chopped parsley, instead of dill.

PEPPERS CAPRICCIO

Frying peppers are now a commonplace item in most Italian restaurants, and when in season are readily available under that name in most supermarkets.

8 large green frying peppers
¼ cup olive oil
1 large onion, thinly sliced
3 cloves garlic, finely minced (1½ teaspoons)
3 tablespoons fresh basil, chopped, or 3 teaspoons dried
½ teaspoon salt
¼ teaspoon freshly ground black pepper

Cut off the tops of the peppers. Cut them into quarters, remove the seeds, and trim off the membranes. Heat the olive oil in a large skillet and add the peppers and the onion. Toss to coat with the oil. Cover the skillet and cook over moderate heat for 5 minutes. Add the garlic and continue to cook, covered, for another 10 minutes. Stir occasionally. Remove the cover and add the basil, salt, and black pepper. Sauté, uncovered, for another 2 minutes. The peppers should be fork tender but not soft. Serve chilled as part of an antipasto. These are also delicious as a hot vegetable with sautéed veal or a broiled steak. *Serves 6 to 8.*

STUFFED PEPPERS PASSETTO

Many years ago *Life* magazine ran a monthly feature on the great restaurants of the world, which was later incorporated into a book. All the full-color pictures were mouth-watering, but for me the most unforgettable was that of the table at Passetto in Rome. As soon as my husband and I reached Rome, we headed for Passeto's, camera in hand; I explained that we wanted to take our own pictures because we had been so tantalized by those in *Life.* We soon realized that they thought we too were from *Life.* In addition to everything we had ordered, we were offered a nibble of everything the kitchen was preparing for others. I found the stuffed peppers and the Roman-style Stuffed Tomatoes (see index) especially memorable. This recipe is my own re-creation.

> 4 small green bell peppers (about 1 pound)
> 1 7-ounce can Italian tuna fish
> 4 cloves garlic, minced (2 teaspoons)
> 2 tablespoons pitted and finely chopped oil-cured olives
> 1 cup fresh bread crumbs
> ¼ cup finely minced parsley
> ½ teaspoon salt
> ½ teaspoon dried basil
> ¼ teaspoon freshly ground black pepper
> 1 egg, lightly beaten
> ½ cup olive oil

Preheat oven to 375°. Cut off the tops of the peppers, scoop out the seeds, and cut out the membranes. Combine the tuna fish, garlic, chopped olives, bread crumbs, parsley, salt, basil, pepper, and egg. Use this mixture to stuff the peppers. Pour the olive oil into an ovenproof dish and place the peppers in the oil. Baste with some of the oil, and bake for 30 minutes, basting every 10 minutes with oil.

Let them cool to room temperature. They may be prepared as long as 2 days in advance, cooled, and refrigerated. Bring them to room temperature before serving. If you are serving these as part of a large assortment of hors d'oeuvres, cut each pepper in half. *Makes 4 to 8.*

STUFFED PEPPERS SOUTHERN STYLE

Use 4 small red sweet peppers. With a mortar and pestle, crush 2 cloves garlic and 4 anchovies, mashing them into a smooth paste. Transfer the mixture to a medium-sized bowl, and add 2 tablespoons chopped capers, 2 tablespoons white raisins, 2 tablespoons pine nuts, ¼ cup finely chopped parsley, ¼ cup grated Parmesan cheese, ¼ teaspoon freshly ground black pepper, 1 cup bread crumbs, and ¾ cup olive oil. Mix well and taste for salt. Cut the peppers in half lengthwise and fill each half with the mixture. Pour ½ cup olive oil into a baking pan and carefully place the peppers in it. Bake for 20 minutes, basting once. *Makes 8.*

ROMAN-STYLE STUFFED TOMATOES

These tomatoes are a good addition to an antipasto, and the small, rather hard variety we usually pass by when making a salad lend themselves perfectly to this treatment. I have found that when you bake the tomatoes long enough to cook the rice, they tend to fall apart, so I recommend partial precooking of the rice.

6 small firm tomatoes
12 tablespoons olive oil
6 cloves garlic, finely minced (1 tablespoon)
6 tablespoons finely minced parsley
¾ cup rice
1½ cups chicken broth
3 tablespoons pine nuts
1½ teaspoons dried basil
1½ teaspoons dried oregano
1½ teaspoons salt
¼ teaspoon freshly ground black pepper
6 tablespoons freshly grated Parmesan cheese

Cut off about ½ inch at the stem end of the tomatoes. Reserve the tops. Carefully scoop out the pulp and rub it through a strainer to remove the seeds. Reserve the strained pulp. Sprinkle the inside of the tomatoes with a pinch of salt and let them drain upside down for 15 minutes. Meanwhile heat 6 tablespoons of the olive oil in a small saucepan and sauté the garlic and parsley for 2 minutes. Add the rice and continue to sauté for 5 minutes, stirring constantly to coat the rice with the oil. Add the chicken broth, 6 tablespoons of the reserved tomato pulp, the pine nuts, basil, oregano, salt, and pepper. Bring to a boil, cover, and simmer for 20 minutes. The rice should still be *al dente*. Add the cheese and mix well. Let the rice cool a bit.

Preheat oven to 400°. Stuff each tomato shell with some of the rice and put its top in place. Place the stuffed tomatoes in an oiled baking dish. Brush the surface of each tomato with 1 tablespoon of the remaining olive oil and bake for 20 minutes. Serve at room temperature, or refrigerate and bring to room temperature before scrving. Plates and forks are necessary. *Makes 6 servings.*

GENOESE STUFFED TOMATOES

Preheat oven to 350°. Prepare the tomatoes as in the main recipe. Combine 2¼ cups cooked rice (preferably Italian Arborio) with 6 tablespoons Pesto Sauce (see index), and the reserved tomato pulp, and carefully stuff the tomato shells with the mixture. Put the tops back on the tomatoes. Pour 4 tablespoons of olive oil into a baking dish just large enough to hold the tomatoes. Place them in the dish and brush each with 1 tablespoon of olive oil. Bake for 30 minutes. *Makes 6 servings.*

STUFFED ZUCCHINI

Although this is usually served hot, I find it even more flavorful at room temperature. When the wedges are arranged like spokes with a tomato rose in the center, the effect is that of a huge flower.

3 medium zucchini (about 1½ pounds)
½ cup olive oil
¾ cup finely chopped onion
2 cloves garlic, finely chopped (1 teaspoon)
½ pound prosciutto, finely diced
½ cup fine bread crumbs
1½ teaspoons dried basil
2 tablespoons finely minced parsley
½ teaspoon salt
¼ teaspoon freshly ground black pepper
10 tablespoons freshly grated Parmesan cheese
1 egg, beaten

Preheat oven to 350°. Parboil the zucchini in a large skillet for 4 minutes. Remove to paper towels and cool. Cut in half lengthwise. Scoop out the pulp with a melon-baller. Chop and drain the pulp. In a medium-sized skillet, heat ¼ cup of the olive oil and sauté the onion until it is transparent. Add the zucchini pulp, garlic, prosciutto, bread crumbs, basil, parsley, salt, pepper, and 4 tablespoons of the cheese. Remove from the heat and let cool for 10 minutes. Stir in the beaten egg. Stuff the zucchini shells with this mixture and sprinkle the tops with the remaining 6 tablespoons of cheese. Pour a few drops of olive oil on the tops. Pour the remaining olive oil into a baking pan and place the stuffed zucchini in the oil. Bake for 40 minutes, basting every 10 minutes. Cool and then refrigerate, covered. When ready to serve, remove from the refrigerator and let come to room temperature. Cut the boats in halves or thirds and decorate each piece with a carrot flower. *Makes 6 to 9 servings.*

SEASONED NUTS

Nuts are always a convenient item for the cocktail hour. Rather than serving the ubiquitous peanuts or the more interesting but far more expensive seasoned nuts, why not make seasoned nuts yourself? In a tightly sealed container, they will keep for weeks in the refrigerator, or they may be frozen and thawed overnight in the refrigerator or for a few hours at room temperature.

A jelly-roll pan is best for baking the nuts, as the sides prevent the butter from dripping; for the quantities in these recipes a cake pan or pie plate would be too small.

HERB-PEPPER ALMONDS

Blanched almonds are available in any supermarket in cans or cellophane bags.

> 6 tablespoons butter
> 2 cups blanched almonds
> 4 teaspoons Herb Pepper Seasoning (Spice Islands)
> kosher salt

Preheat oven to 350°. Melt the butter in a jelly-roll pan in the oven. Stir in the almonds and Herb Pepper Seasoning. Make sure the nuts are well coated. Bake 20 minutes, stirring every 5 minutes. Sprinkle with kosher salt and toast 5 more minutes. Drain on paper towels. Serve warm or cold.

CURRIED NUTS
Instead of the Herb Pepper Seasoning, add 2 tablespoons curry powder, 1 teaspoon ground ginger, and 1 teaspoon Worcestershire Sauce. Other nuts may be used instead of almonds.

CHILIED PEANUTS

> 2 cups unsalted roasted peanuts
> 6 tablespoons butter
> 1 tablespoon chili powder
> kosher salt

Proceed as in preceding recipe but bake only 10 minutes.

DEVILED PECANS

4 tablespoons butter
¼ cup Worcestershire sauce
10 dashes Tabasco
4 cups pecan halves
3 tablespoons garlic salt

Preheat oven to 300°. Melt the butter in a jelly-roll pan in the oven. Remove pan from oven and stir in the Worcestershire sauce and Tabasco. Add the pecans and stir to coat them. Return to the oven for 10 minutes. Sprinkle with the garlic salt and bake 5 minutes more. Spread on paper towels to drain and cool.

ITALIAN PECANS

Put 2 cups pecan halves into a jelly-roll pan. Pour 6 tablespoons melted butter over them and stir. Sprinkle with 1 tablespoon Italian herb seasoning and 2 teaspoons garlic powder. Turn them with a large spoon so that the seasonings are distributed. Roast 20 minutes. Drain on paper towels and sprinkle with kosher salt.

ELLEN'S ROASTED PECANS

These take time but not much attention.

4 cups pecan halves
¼ pound butter, melted
kosher salt

Preheat oven to 200°. Put the pecans in a jelly-roll pan and roast them for 30 minutes. Pour over the melted butter and sprinkle with a little kosher salt. Stir well to ensure that all sides are well coated. Roast for another 4 hours, turning them every hour. Drain on paper towels. Serve warm or cooled.

MEXICAN WALNUTS

4 cups walnut halves
½ stick butter, melted (¼ cup)
1 tablespoon chili powder
2 teaspoons powdered cumin seed
kosher salt

Preheat oven to 350°. Put the walnuts in a jelly-roll pan. Pour the melted butter on them and stir to coat them. Bake for 15 minutes. Sprinkle with the chili powder and cumin seed and stir well to distribute the seasonings. Bake an additional 10 minutes. Drain on paper towels and sprinkle with kosher salt.

WALNUTS TERYAKI

2 cups walnut halves
¼ cup soy sauce
2 tablespoons dry sherry
2 tablespoons sesame oil
1 clove garlic, crushed
1 teaspoon ground ginger
2 dashes Tabasco sauce
1 tablespoon brown sugar
kosher salt

Preheat oven to 350°. Put the walnuts in a jelly-roll pan. In a small saucepan, combine the soy sauce, sherry, sesame oil, garlic, ginger, Tabasco, and brown sugar. Heat for a minute to dissolve the sugar. Pour over the walnuts and stir to coat them. Bake for 20 minutes. Put on paper towels to drain and sprinkle lightly with kosher salt.

Cold Seafood

While Americans are generally reputed to dislike fish, there is one notable exception—cold shrimp served with a spicy red sauce. Until the recent sharp increase in the price of shrimp, this was a must as cocktail fare. However awe-inspiring a bowl of chilled Beluga caviar may be, many of us can make do with other uncooked offerings of the waters. My own favorite is freshly opened clams or oysters *au naturel*, with only a squirt of lemon and a few grinds of pepper; for those who share this preference, either is a refreshing drink accompaniment.

Many kinds of smoked fish are available either in local stores or from reputable mail-order sources. Most people know smoked salmon—Alaskan, Nova Scotia, Scottish, or Irish—but appetizer departments now stock many other kinds of smoked or kippered fish, among them sturgeon, whitefish, trout, eel, and sablefish. (When serving these as cocktail party fare, make sure the fish is boned.) Thinly sliced, buttered pumpernickel, rye bread, toast, or, of course, bagels, with capers, onion slices, or lemon wedges, are all perfect accompaniments. Although guests can make their own open-face sandwiches, plates and forks are welcome adjuncts. Many other ready-to-eat varieties of fish can be served merely by opening a can—tuna fillets; sardines; herring; smoked shrimp, clams, and oysters; and the versatile anchovy. Most of them are good alone or garnished merely with chopped parsley and lemon.

Most fish and shellfish, however, require some sort of preliminary cooking, even when they are to be served cold. Shrimp, mussels, and scallops must be lightly poached even if they are to be served with a sauce, although scallops and many types of fish can be "cooked" without heat, as evidenced by that wonderful Latin-American creation *Seviche*, in which they are marinated in lemon or lime juice. (See index.)

One can transform many varieties of seafood into something more special, such as a pâté or mousse. Even though seafood is extremely perishable, such dishes can often be prepared a day in advance.

CRAB SPREAD

1 teaspoon dried tarragon
¼ cup lemon juice
1 cup fresh crabmeat (about ¼ pound), or
   1 6½-ounce can Geisha brand
½ teaspoon salt
2 dashes Tabasco
1 teaspoon Worcestershire sauce
¼ teaspoon dry mustard
¼ teaspoon celery seed
3 ounces cream cheese
¼ cup heavy cream
1 teaspoon onion juice
2 tablespoons finely chopped chives
1 tablespoon finely chopped parsley

Soak the tarragon in the lemon juice for 10 minutes. Flake crabmeat and remove any tendons. (If using canned crabmeat, rinse under cold water and dry thoroughly on paper towels.) Place the crabmeat in a bowl; add the lemon juice and tarragon, and the salt, Tabasco, Worcestershire sauce, dry mustard, and celery seed. Cover bowl tightly with plastic wrap and marinate in the refrigerator at least 2 hours or overnight. Let the cream cheese soften to room temperature. With an electric mixer or a food processor, cream the cheese, gradually adding the heavy cream. Drain off the liquid from the crab mixture and add the crab to the cheese. Stir in the onion juice, chives, and parsley. Chill. Can be used to fill artichoke bottoms or cucumber cups or served as a spread with crackers or melba toast. Also excellent spread on toast rounds, sprinkled with Gruyère and heated for 5 minutes. *Makes 1 cup.*

CRAB-CUCUMBER SPREAD

Peel, seed, and chop 3 cucumbers. Set them in a strainer over a bowl and let them drain for ½ hour. Bring 4 ounces cream cheese to room temperature. In a large bowl combine cucumbers, cream cheese, canned crabmeat, 6 tablespoons minced onion, 1 teaspoon grated lemon peel, ¼ cup soy sauce, 2 dashes Tabasco, ⅓ cup mayonnaise, and 2 tablespoons chopped dill. Chill 4 hours or overnight. *Makes about 2½ cups.*

CURRIED CRABMEAT

Soften 4 ounces cream cheese. Combine with ½ cup mayonnaise, ¼ cup sour cream, 1½ teaspoons Worcestershire sauce, 2 dashes Tabasco, and 2 teaspoons curry powder and mix until smooth. Stir in 2 6½-ounce cans crabmeat, ½ cup coarsely chopped macadamia nuts, and ¼ pound coarsely chopped, cooked shrimp. *Makes about 4 cups.*

OSLO FISH SPREAD

Even herring haters will take to this—and have trouble identifying the main ingredient.

    2 3¼-ounce cans kipper snacks
    3 ounces cream cheese, softened to room temperature
    1 tablespoon lemon juice
    6 dashes Tabasco
    3 tablespoons grated onion
    1 tablespoon chopped parsley
    1 tablespoon chopped chives

Drain the kippers and mash them in a bowl. Add the rest of the ingredients and stir thoroughly to combine. Chill for at least 1 hour or up to 2 days. Serve with pumpernickel crackers or squares of pumpernickel bread. *Makes 1⅓ cups.*

HERRING SALAD

1 8-ounce jar herring in wine sauce
1 cup finely chopped, unpeeled red apple
4 ounces cream cheese
¾ cup finely chopped red onion
4 tablespoons chopped fresh dill
¼ teaspoon sugar
3 tablespoons sour cream
2 hard-cooked egg yolks, sieved

Drain the herring, reserving the juice but discarding the onions. Marinate the apple in the herring juice. Let the cream cheese soften to room temperature. Cut the herring bits into ½-inch pieces. Combine with the cream cheese, onion, 3 tablespoons of the dill, the sugar, and the sour cream. Drain the apple and fold in. Chill, covered, for a few hours or overnight. Mound the spread on a plate and decorate with the remaining tablespoon of dill and the sieved egg yolks. Surround the mound with squares of dark pumpernickel—Danish pumpernickel if you can obtain it. *Makes 2 cups.*

HOW TO PREPARE MUSSELS

Appreciated by most Europeans, mussels have yet to attain much popularity in this country. Consequently, they are relatively inexpensive—they have been called the "poor man's oyster." Their main drawback is the work involved in preparing them.

Scrub off the seaweed, barnacles, stones, and other foreign appendages that cling to the mussel shells. Then pull off the so-called beards—rubber gloves and a stiff wire brush will make this task easier. Soak mussels in a bowl of cold water with about ¼ cup cornmeal for 1 to 2 hours, then drain, scrub again, and rinse thoroughly in cold water. Put mussels in a large saucepan with ½ bay leaf and ½ cup to 1 cup white wine for 1 quart mussels and any additional ingredients specified in the particular recipe. Cover, bring to a boil, lower the heat, and simmer 2 or 3 minutes. By this time the mussels should have opened; discard any that have not. Proceed according to recipe.

If fresh mussels are not available, canned ones packed in brine (found in specialty stores) may be substituted, although the texture is not as firm as that of the fresh ones. Rinse canned mussels, drain, and dry carefully on paper towels.

PICKLED MUSSELS

1 quart fresh mussels (about 2½ pounds)
½ cup white wine
½ bay leaf

MARINADE
1 onion, thinly sliced (1 cup)
2 cloves garlic, crushed (1 teaspoon)
½ cup tarragon wine vinegar
½ cup Chablis
2 tablespoons olive oil
1 tablespoon chopped shallots
1 bay leaf
1 tablespoon chopped parsley
6 peppercorns
¼ teaspoon dry mustard
¼ teaspoon dried tarragon

Clean and steam the mussels according to the preceding instructions. Combine the marinade ingredients and the strained broth and heat to the boiling point. Remove from heat. When the mussels are cool enough to handle, remove them from their shells and place them in a heatproof bowl. Pour the marinade over them and chill overnight or up to 4 days. To serve, remove the mussels and onion slices from the marinade. Serve in a bowl, surrounded by small squares of pumpernickel. *Makes about 2 cups.*

NEW ORLEANS MUSSELS

1 quart fresh mussels, or 1 15½-ounce can
⅓ cup mayonnaise
2 tablespoons finely chopped parsley
1 tablespoon finely chopped shallots
1 tablespoon finely chopped chives
1 teaspoon chopped capers
½ teaspoon dried tarragon
½ teaspoon Creole Mustard *
2 cloves garlic, finely minced (1 teaspoon)
dash Tabasco
¼ teaspoon salt
1 hard-cooked egg, finely chopped
3 tablespoons finely chopped parsley

Prepare fresh or canned mussels according to preceding instructions. Combine all the other ingredients except the parsley. Fold the mussels into the mayonnaise mixture. Chill for at least 4 hours or overnight. Place in a serving dish and sprinkle with the chopped parsley. Serve with melba toast. *Makes about 2 cups.*

DANISH CURRIED MUSSELS

Although we usually associate curry with Indian food, the Scandinavians, especially the Danish, often use a light curry sauce with smoked fish as well as with a variety of other foods. This mixture is delicious as a spread on Danish pumpernickel bread or as a filling for cucumber cups or artichoke bottoms.

1 quart mussels
1 cup white wine
2 shallots, finely chopped
2 small onions, peeled and quartered
3 sprigs parsley
pinch cayenne pepper

*Creole Mustard can be obtained from Zatarain's, Inc., New Orleans, Louisiana 70114.

½ bay leaf
a 1-inch strip lemon peel
¼ pound medium-sized mushrooms,
   wiped and sliced thin
2 tablespoons lemon juice
3 tablespoons sour cream
3 tablespoons mayonnaise
¾ teaspoon curry powder
¼ cup finely chopped parsley

Prepare the mussels according to preceding instructions, but cook them in 1 cup white wine, along with the shallots, onions, parsley sprigs, cayenne, bay leaf, and lemon peel, over high heat for about 5 minutes, shaking the pan occasionally. (You can strain the resulting broth through a double thickness of cheesecloth and use it when you need fish stock.) Let the mussels cool. Put the mushrooms in a medium-sized bowl and add the lemon juice, tossing to cover them with the juice. Mix the sour cream with the mayonnaise and curry powder. Remove the mussels from their shells (you should have about ½ pound of mussels). Add them to the mushrooms, pour over the curry sauce, and toss to coat well. Cover and refrigerate for several hours. Sprinkle with chopped parsley before serving. *Makes 2 cups.*

SMOKED OYSTER SPREAD

8 ounces cream cheese
2 3⅔-ounce cans smoked oysters
2 teaspoons onion juice
1 clove garlic, crushed
1 tablespoon soy sauce
2 tablespoons lemon juice
2 tablespoons chopped chives

Bring cream cheese to room temperature. Drain the oysters. Place all ingredients in the bowl of an electric blender or a food processor and run for about 1 minute, until all ingredients are blended. Cover and chill. *Makes 1 cup.*

SMOKED SALMON MOUSSE

Versions of this quick but impressive-looking appetizer have recently been appearing in almost every magazine concerned with food. I suspect that its rediscovery relates to the popularity of food processors, but I have made it in a blender for years with just as happy results.

½ pound smoked salmon
3 tablespoons lemon juice
¼ pound butter, melted
¾ cup sour cream
3 tablespoons finely chopped fresh dill
freshly ground black pepper to taste

GARNISH
thin lemon slices
chopped fresh dill
capers

Coarsely chop the salmon. Place in a blender or food processor, add the lemon juice, and purée. With the machine on, add the melted butter in a steady stream, scraping the sides of the container occasionally. Place the salmon mixture in a small bowl and stir in the sour cream and chopped dill. Taste for seasoning—it will probably need only a few grindings of pepper. Spoon the mousse into a 2-cup soufflé dish or other serving dish. Cover securely with plastic wrap. Refrigerate for at least 4 hours or up to 2 days. When ready to serve, decorate the top with twists of the lemon slices, sprinkling the chopped dill between. Put a small cluster of capers in the center of the dish. Serve with melba toast. *Fills a 2-cup soufflé dish.*

LOX SPREAD

Lox is a saltier, less expensive version of Nova Scotia smoked salmon, which can be substituted if you cannot obtain lox, though you will probably have to add salt.

½ pound lox, chopped
4 ounces whipped chive cream cheese
2 tablespoons onion juice
1 tablespoon lemon juice
¼ teaspoon freshly ground black pepper
2 tablespoons chopped fresh dill

In the container of an electric blender or a food processor put the lox, cheese, onion juice, lemon juice, and pepper. Blend, stopping occasionally to push the mixture into the blades. Place in a bowl and stir in the dill. Chill. Serve with squares of pumpernickel bread or Scandinavian crisp bread. *Makes 1 cup.*

NOVA SCOTIA SALMON ROLLS

8 ounces cream cheese, softened to room temperature
3 tablespoons onion juice
6 tablespoons chopped fresh dill
6 dashes Tabasco
½ pound sliced Nova Scotia salmon
salmon caviar (optional)

Put the cream cheese in a bowl and add the onion juice, dill, and Tabasco. With a large spoon, blend all the ingredients until you have a smooth paste. Cut each slice of salmon into 2 or 3 pieces, across the width, to produce slices about 2 by 2½ inches. Spread each slice with the cheese mixture and roll it up jelly-roll fashion. Place the rolls on a serving plattter, seam side down, cover with plastic wrap, and chill for 2 hours or overnight. Just before serving, place a sprig of dill in one end of the roll. If you wish, add salmon caviar to the spread, or dip one end of each roll into it. *Makes about 24.*

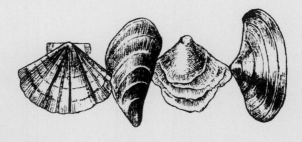

SEVICHE

This dish, originating "south of the border," is gaining popularity here. The recipe allows endless variations, the only constant being that the fish is marinated in some sort of citrus juice for a few hours. This steeping "cooks" the fish, and it loses its translucence and firms up in texture. Most Mexican versions use various kinds of native white fish, but I prefer bay scallops—impeccably fresh. Seviche makes a perfect main course for a summer luncheon.

1 pound bay scallops
1 cup lime juice
½ cup thinly sliced red onion, slices cut in quarters
1 heaping tablespoon seeded, chopped green chilies
½ cup peeled, seeded, and chopped tomato
2 tablespoons chopped parsley
2 cloves garlic, chopped (1 teaspoon)
½ teaspoon salt
2 tablespoons olive oil
1 medium avocado, peeled and cubed
1 15-ounce can whole-kernel young sweet corn (available in
   Chinese and German stores), drained
2 tablespoons chopped fresh coriander (cilantro)
   or fresh parsley

Put the scallops into a glass bowl and pour the lime juice over them. Cover and refrigerate at least 4 hours or overnight. Drain off the lime juice and reserve it. Add to the scallops the onion, chilies, tomato, parsley, garlic, salt, olive oil, avocado, and 2 tablespoons of the reserved lime juice. Stir well to blend all ingredients, cover tightly, and refrigerate again for at least 2 hours or up to 8 hours. When ready to serve, stir in the corn. Using a slotted spoon, fill the serving dish. Sprinkle with the coriander or parsley. *Serves 6 to 8.*

SHRIMP COCKTAIL

This all-time favorite is too often poorly prepared. There are two rules for dealing with any type of seafood: make sure it is fresh and do not overcook it.

3 cups water
½ cup dry light vermouth
1 stalk celery and leaves, about ½ cup
2 small onions, coarsely chopped (½ cup)
juice of 1 lemon (½ cup)
1 teaspoon salt
½ teaspoon freshly ground pepper
½ bay leaf
4 sprigs parsley
2 cloves garlic, crushed (1 teaspoon)
¼ teaspoon dried thyme
1 pound shrimp (about 25 to 30)

Put all the ingredients except the shrimp into a large saucepan. Bring to a boil, lower the heat, and simmer 20 minutes. Add the shrimp, return to a boil, lower the heat, and simmer about 4 minutes. Drain, cool, shell, and devein. Chill in a covered container until ready to serve. They may be poached a day in advance. Serve on a plate with a scallop shell of the desired sauce in the center. *Serves 6 to 8 when accompanied by other dishes.*

DIP FOR SHRIMP

Sauces for shrimp cocktails are most often based on a mixture of catchup or chili sauce with horseradish. For my taste, sauces of this potent nature overwhelm the delicate flavor of the shrimp; I prefer this gentler dip. Velvety Cocktail Sauce, Tartare Sauce, and Remoulade Sauce (see index) are also good accompaniments.

½ cup mayonnaise
2 tablespoons Escoffier Sauce Diable (available in jars)
4 teaspoons finely chopped fresh chives

Combine all ingredients and serve separately. *Makes about ½ cup.*

SHRIMP PASTE

An Americanization of the famous English potted shrimp, which we cannot really duplicate here, since we do not have the tiny shrimp required.

 ¾ pound cooked shrimp, coarsely chopped
 ¼ teaspoon mace
 1 clove garlic, crushed (½ teaspoon)
 ¾ teaspoon lemon juice
 1 teaspoon finely chopped fresh dill
 ⅛ teaspoon dry mustard
 ¼ teaspoon salt
 pinch freshly ground black pepper
 6 tablespoons butter, softened

Purée everything but the butter in a blender. Then combine with the softened butter. Cover tightly with plastic wrap and chill for 8 hours or overnight. Serve with melba toast. *Makes 1½ cups.*

SHRIMP PÂTÉ

When one thinks of pâtés, meat or poultry combinations usually come to mind, but fish pâtés are gaining favor. This one with shrimp as the main ingredient provides a pleasing change. The tiny aluminum-foil loaf pans available in most supermarkets make handy containers.

 1 pound shrimp, cooked, shelled, deveined, and coarsely cut
 5 tablespoons softened butter, cut into 5 pieces
 1 tablespoon finely chopped shallots
 2 tablespoons dry sherry
 1 teaspoon salt
 ¼ teaspoon freshly ground white pepper
 ½ teaspoon dry mustard
 2 teaspoons dried tarragon

4 whole cooked shrimp
2 capers
parsley or watercress
4 lemon cups
Green Mayonnaise (see index)

Preheat oven to 350°. Place the shrimp and the butter in the bowl of an electric food processor or blender and run the machine for 1 minute. Add the shallots, sherry, salt, white pepper, dry mustard, and tarragon, and run another 30 seconds to combine the ingredients. Grease a 2-cup loaf pan. Spread the shrimp mixture in the pan and bake 20 minutes. Remove and let cool. Cover tightly and refrigerate overnight. Turn out on a platter. Cut the 4 whole cooked shrimp in half lengthwise. At each end of the pâté place pieces of 2 shrimp around a caper to form a flower. Surround the pâté with parsley or watercress. Fill the lemon cups with Green Mayonnaise and nestle 2 of them on each side. Serve with melba toast made from thin-sliced whole wheat bread. *Fills a 2-cup loaf pan.*

TUNA SPREAD

1 7-ounce can Italian tuna fish, drained
2 tablespoons minced onion
2 tablespoons Pernod
2 tablespoons mayonnaise
2 tablespoons sour cream
¼ teaspoon freshly ground black pepper
3 dashes Tabasco
1 cup grated sharp Cheddar cheese (¼ pound)
1 tablespoon finely minced fresh dill
½ cup finely chopped pimiento-stuffed olives

Place the tuna fish, onion, Pernod, mayonnaise, sour cream, pepper, Tabasco, and cheese in the container of an electric blender or food processor. Blend at high speed. Stop after a minute and scrape contents from sides toward blades. Blend another minute. Put into a bowl. Stir in the dill and olives. Chill. Serve with raw vegetables or crackers. *Makes 1½ cups.*

TUNA MOUSSE

1 envelope gelatin
3 tablespoons dry sherry
6 ounces cream cheese, softened
1 7-ounce can tuna in oil, well drained
2 hard-cooked eggs, chopped
1 tablespoon finely minced onion
6 dashes Tabasco
1 teaspoon Worcestershire sauce
¾ teaspoon prepared horseradish
¼ teaspoon salt
¼ cup chopped scallions

GARNISH
pimiento-stuffed green olives, sliced
chopped parsley

Sprinkle the gelatin over the sherry and heat in a small saucepan to dissolve the gelatin. Place all the other ingredients except the scallions in a blender or food processor. Blend until quite smooth. Pour in the gelatin mixture and blend for another 2 minutes to be sure it is incorporated. Pour the mixture into a bowl and fold in the scallions. Pour into a serving dish and cover with plastic wrap to prevent a crust from forming. Chill 12 hours. Decorate with olive slices around the edges and a circle of chopped parsley in the center. *Makes 1½ cups.*

CAVIAR MOUSSE

This is my drop-dead hors d'oeuvre. I never hesitate to serve it over again to the same guests, since they often ask for it if I don't. It has two distinct advantages over the usual caviar mousse: a more attractive appearance and a smaller cost. Please do not be put off by the number of pots and pans required; the applause of your guests will be your reward. You won't want to undertake this for one couple dropping by for a quick drink, but for VIP guests it is the perfect offering.

2 eggs, separated, plus 1 egg white
¼ cup cold water
1 envelope gelatin
¾ cup heavy cream, plus 2 tablespoons
4 ounces cream cheese with chives
1½ teaspoons grated lemon rind
2 tablespoons lemon juice
½ teaspoon salt
¼ teaspoon white pepper
4 shallots, crushed in a press (2 teaspoons)
1 3½-ounce jar Danish black lumpfish caviar
1 cup chopped fresh chives
1 small jar pimientos

Put the 3 egg whites into a bowl of an electric mixer and the 2 yolks into a saucepan. Put the cold water into a Pyrex measuring cup and sprinkle the gelatin over the water. Place the cup in a skillet containing 1 inch of simmering water to dissolve the gelatin. Beat the ¾ cup cream until stiff. Place in the refrigerator. Press the cream cheese through a sieve. Beat the whites until stiff. Add the 2 tablespoons of heavy cream to the egg yolks and beat with a whisk over a low flame until mixture thickens. Pour into a large mixing bowl. Add the gelatin and slowly stir in the cream cheese. Stir in the lemon rind, lemon juice, salt, pepper, and shallots. Fold in the whipped cream and the egg whites. Pour into a 5-inch, 2½-cup soufflé dish. Refrigerate at least 2 hours, or preferably overnight.

About 1 hour before serving, unmold the mousse onto a plate. Using a blunt knife, spread the caviar over the top and sides and surround the base with the chives. Drain and dry the pimientos. Using a truffle cutter or aspic cutter, make seven cutouts, using three or four shapes. Make a circle of six cutouts around the rim of the top and place one in the center. Serve with melba toast. *Fills a 2½-cup mold.*

RED CAVIAR MOUSSE

Now that salmon caviar has escalated in price this has become the rich relative of the preceding mousse.

    2 teaspoons vegetables oil
    4 eggs, separated
    1 3-ounce package cream cheese with chives
    ½ cup cold water
    2 envelopes gelatin
    1¼ cups milk
    3 tablespoons butter
    3 tablespoons flour
    2 teaspoons grated lemon peel
    3 tablespoons finely chopped fresh dill
    2 tablespoons finely chopped chives
    ¼ teaspoon freshly ground black pepper
    2 tablespoons juice of grated onion
    ⅔ cup heavy cream
    1 8-ounce jar salmon caviar

With a pastry brush, lightly oil a 4-cup mold (preferably fish-shaped). Turn the oiled mold upside down and let it drain on several thicknesses of paper towels. Place the 4 egg whites in a mixing bowl and 3 of the yolks in a small bowl (reserve the extra yolk for another use). Push the cream cheese through a sieve. Put the water in a Pyrex cup, sprinkle the gelatin over it, and place the cup in a small skillet containing 1 inch of simmering water to dissolve the gelatin. Heat the milk. Melt the butter in the top of a double boiler over simmering water. Remove from heat and stir in the flour, using a wire whisk to prevent lumping. Gradually pour in the hot milk, stirring constantly. Return to the heat, bring to a boil, reduce heat, and simmer 5 minutes, stirring about every minute. Remove from the heat, stir in the gelatin, and stir 1 or 2 minutes, making sure that the gelatin dissolves. Stir in the cheese, the 3 egg yolks, the lemon peel, dill, chives, pepper, and onion juice. Place the mixture in a bowl and put into the refrigerator for about ½ hour or until the mixture begins to thicken and set around the edges. Whip the heavy cream until it is firm but not stiff. Beat the egg whites until they are stiff but not dry. Fold the cream and then the egg whites into the mixture. Fold in the caviar carefully so as not to break the eggs. Pour the mixture into the oiled mold, cover with plastic wrap, and refrigerate at least 6 hours or overnight. Unmold onto a platter.

You can decorate this with watercress and Nova Scotia Salmon Rolls (see index). If you are using a fish-shaped mold, you can use a slice of pimiento-stuffed green olive to form the fish's eye and slivers of green pepper on the tail to indicate striations. Serve with English water biscuits (Carr's or Jacob's) or melba toast. *Fills a 4-cup mold.*

CRAIG CLAIBORNE'S SALMON MOUSSE

Many recipes for salmon mousse call for freshly poached salmon and much grinding and sieving, but this one is not only simple and quick but just as delicious as the more time-consuming versions.

1 envelope gelatin
2 tablespoons lemon juice
1 small slice onion
½ cup boiling water
½ cup mayonnaise
¼ teaspoon paprika
1 teaspoon dried dill
1 1-pound can salmon, drained
1 cup heavy cream

Empty the envelope of gelatin into the container of an electric blender or a food processor (see note). Add the lemon juice, onion slice, and boiling water. Place the cover on the container, turn the motor to high speed, and blend ingredients for 40 seconds. Turn the motor off. Add the mayonnaise, paprika, dill, and salmon. Cover and blend at high speed. Remove the cover and add the cream, one third at a time, blending for a few seconds after each addition. Blend for 30 seconds longer. Pour into a 4-cup mold. Chill. Unmold onto a platter. If you are using a fish-shaped mold, decorate as described in the preceding recipe. Surround with scored cucumber rounds, each topped with a tiny shrimp and a caper. *Fills a 4-cup mold.*

Note: This recipe was written before the advent of food processors; if you use one, cut down the length of time you run the machine. Recently the price of canned salmon has skyrocketed and 1-pound cans have shrunk to 15½ ounces, but this does not affect the recipe.

Cold
Meats and Poultry

As the following recipes show, cold-meat hors d'oeuvres encompass much more than the offerings of a delicatessen. For a large cocktail party, however, you may want to provide cold cuts, sausages, breads, mustards, and pickles. Unusual cold cuts can be found in great variety in ethnic markets. Salami—Italian, German, Hungarian, or Jewish—is a favorite in any language. Polish and Hungarian kielbasa come already cooked and can be served in chunks or slices. Summer sausage, cervelat, Lebanon bologna, Italian pepperoni, and German bierwurst and yachtwurst are widely available. Liverwurst and braunschweiger are old standbys; you can also try their spreadable cousins teawurst and mettwurst. In German stores one can purchase excellent head cheese and *Sulze*, that jellied, vinegary delight that can be served in slices or cubes, and tossed with an onion-flavored vinaigrette, as well as *Lachschinken* and smoked pork loin. Scandinavian stores sometimes have a spicy veal, *rullespølse*, which is well worth searching for.

With a little time and effort, you can convert many of these items into tantalizing finger foods.

Note: The prepackaged cold cuts found in supermarkets are to be avoided; they are usually either bland or blatantly oversalted.

STEAK TARTARE

While this makes a fine luncheon or supper dish, it is also perfect cocktail party fare, especially when you want something substantial to help your guests keep their equilibrium. There are as many ver-

73

sions as there are cooks: some add whole eggs or egg yolks, anchovies, capers, cognac, olive oil. I prefer to omit additives and offer small bowls of capers, anchovies, and extra chopped onion on the side. You can form the meat mixture into small balls and roll them in chopped parsley, but a huge log sprinkled with parsley is just as attractive and less trouble. Grind the meat or have it ground as close to serving time as possible—not the day before.

1 pound extra-lean top round of beef, ground twice
2 tablespoons very finely grated onion
2 cloves garlic, crushed (1 teaspoon)
1¼ teaspoons salt
2 teaspoons dry mustard
½ teaspoon freshly ground black pepper
½ cup finely chopped parsley

GARNISHES
1 2-ounce can flat anchovies, coarsely chopped
½ cup capers
½ cup finely chopped onions

Combine all the ingredients except the garnishes. Form the meat into a rectangular loaf. Place it on the long side of a rectangular platter. Line up small bowls of anchovies, capers, and onions in front of the meat and intersperse them with cherry tomato roses and pitted ripe olives. Cover any open spaces with chicory or watercress. Serve with thin slices of pumpernickel, salty rye, buttered toast or melba toast, or 3-inch stalks of celery. *Makes 1 cup.*

CARPACCIO

Slices of raw beef served with a piquant mayonnaise sauce are rapidly overtaking Steak Tartare as a favorite appetizer in restaurants. Said to have originated at Harry's Bar in Venice, carpaccio, like its cooked cousin *fondue bourguignonne*, seems to marry well with a wide range of spicy sauces and can easily be adapted to the cocktail hour. Place the sliced beef on a large chilled platter and surround it with bowls of any desired sauces. Provide plates and forks and let your guests create their own combinations. Do not slice the meat too far in advance as it tends to darken. (Carpaccio is said to have derived its name from the Venetian painter, who was fond of painting in vivid reds.) If you slice the meat when it is partly frozen, it will be easier to produce slender slivers.

> 1 pound raw fillet of beef, sliced almost paper thin
>   and cut into 2-inch lengths

Serve with Watercress Sauce and/or a choice of highly seasoned mayonnaises (see index). *Makes about 12 slices.*

Watercress Sauce

> 3 ounces cream cheese, softened to room temperature
> 1 cup chopped watercress (about 1 bunch, stems removed)
> 1 tablespoon heavy cream

Combine all ingredients and chill.

ROAST BEEF ROLLS

These can be made a day ahead.

> 3 ounces cream cheese, softened to room temperature
> 2 tablespoons chopped red onion
> 1 tablespoon chives, finely chopped
> 2 teaspoons Durkee Sauce
> 1 small clove garlic, crushed
> ½ teaspoon salt
> ¼ teaspoon freshly ground black pepper
> ¼ pound rare roast beef, sliced ⅛-inch thick,
>   each slice 6 by 3½ inches

Place the cream cheese in a bowl, and mix in the onion, chives, Durkee sauce, garlic, salt, and pepper. Spread a portion on each slice of roast beef. Roll up the slices jelly-roll fashion, starting at the long edge. Place on a plate seam side down, cover with plastic wrap, and refrigerate. To serve, cut rolls into 1-inch slices and place a toothpick in each. *Makes 24 slices.*

BOLOGNA FRISBIES

This is a holdover from my teen-age days, and I always underestimate the quantity that will be consumed.

6 ounces cream cheese with chives
8 tablespoons finely minced scallions
1½ teaspoons prepared horseradish
6 slices wide bologna, preferably kosher,
    cut ⅛-inch thick (not quite ½ pound)

Let the cheese soften to room temperature. Mix in the scallions and horseradish. Spread 1 slice of bologna with about a third of the cheese mixture. Cover with another slice, spread again with the cheese mixture, and cover with a third slice. Wrap securely in aluminum foil. Repeat with the other 3 slices. Chill in the refrigerator for a few hours or overnight. When ready to serve, cut each stack into eight wedges, keeping the pies in their original shape. Place a toothpick in each section. *Makes 16 wedges.*

STUFFED HAM ROLLS

These can be made at least a day in advance and stored in the refrigerator. When serving them, place a handful of olives or tiny pickles in the center of a round platter and arrange the rolls radiating out like the spokes of a wheel.

4 ounces grated Cheddar cheese
2 tablespoons butter, at room temperature
5 teaspoons chopped chutney
4 slices boiled ham (¼ pound)
½ cup chopped toasted almonds

Combine the cheese, butter, and chutney. Cut each slice of ham in half, vertically. Spread each slice with the cheese mixture and roll up like a jelly roll. Wrap tightly in foil and chill. Just before serving, cut each roll in half and dip the ends into chopped toasted almonds. *Makes 8 rolls or 16 pieces.*

Can be frozen. Thaw overnight in the refrigerator.

VARIATION

Stuff the ham slices with the cheese mixture for Roquefort Almond Balls (see index). For serving, cut each roll in 3 pieces and put a toothpick in each. *Makes 24 pieces.*

PROSCIUTTO BALLS

¼ pound Bel Paese cheese
¼ pound prosciutto, finely chopped
3 tablespoons chopped chives
¼ teaspoon freshly ground black pepper
thin bread sticks

Let the cheese soften to room temperature. Combine the prosciutto with the cheese, chives, and pepper. Using a measuring teaspoon, form the mixture into balls, rolling them between your palms to shape. They should be about 1 inch in diameter. Place them on a serving plate, cover with plastic wrap, and refrigerate for at least 2 hours. These can be made the day before. Break very thin bread sticks into 2½-inch lengths and stick one in each ball, just before serving. *Makes about 15.*

GENOESE PIES

2 teaspoons Italian herb seasoning
2 tablespoons dry sherry
6 ounces cream cheese, softened to room temperature
¼ teaspoon salt
6 slices Genoa salami

Soak the seasoning in the sherry for 15 minutes, drain, and dry. Combine the cream cheese, seasoning mixture, and salt. Spread a slice of salami with the mixture and cover with another slice. Spread the surface of that slice with more of the mixture and top with still another slice of salami. Wrap securely in aluminum foil and refrigerate. Repeat with the remaining ingredients. Wrap the pies in aluminum foil and refrigerate for at least 4 hours or overnight. When ready to serve, cut each pie into 8 wedges and put a toothpick in each bite. *Makes 16 wedges.*

ITALIAN SALAMI CORNUCOPIAS

These take a bit of time, but with the proper equipment it is easy to turn out a large number. They can be made a day in advance, covered with plastic wrap, and refrigerated or frozen. Thaw them overnight in the refrigerator; do not hoard them too long as the salami tends to darken.

        12 slices (about ¼ pound) Italian hard salami,
            cut in half
        1 egg white, beaten
        1 tablespoon dried basil
        1 tablespoon dried oregano
        ¼ cup dry vermouth
        8 ounces cream cheese, softened at room temperature
        5 tablespoons finely chopped parsley
        ¼ cup finely chopped fresh chives

Place two wire-mesh cake-cooling racks one on top of the other at right angles so they form a grid. Fold a half slice of salami around your finger to form a cornucopia and brush the edges with the egg white. Press edges firmly together and place cornucopia in a square of the grid. Continue to form cornucopias with the rest of the salami. Refrigerate them for 1 hour. Meanwhile soak the basil and oregano in the vermouth for 15 minutes (this will soften the texture and intensify the flavor). Strain the herbs and dry them thoroughly. Combine the cheese with the parsley, chives, basil, and oregano. Fit pastry bag with a No. 5 star tube, fill with the cheese mixture, and pipe some into each cornucopia.

Serve on a platter with Italian olives on a bed of chicory in the center. *Makes 24.*

Can be frozen.

VARIATION

Combine 2 ounces cream cheese with ¼ pound Gorgonzola, at room temperature, ¼ pound fontinella or fontina, finely grated, and 2 tablespoons finely chopped parsley, and use to fill the cornucopias.

MORTADELLA PINWHEELS

Use 8 slices mortadella (about ¼ pound) instead of the salami and double the recipe for the filling. Spread each slice with about 2 tablespoons of the filling and roll tightly, jelly-roll fashion. Wrap the rolls in foil and refrigerate at least 4 hours. When ready to serve, cut each slice into quarters and stick a toothpick in each quarter. *Makes 32.*

GERMAN CHICKEN ROULADE

These miniature golden bites have a surprising, palate-teasing flavor.

2 chicken breasts, boned, skinned, and split
4 slices Westphalian or Black Forest ham
2 ounces Gruyère cheese, thinly sliced
pinch white pepper
¼ teaspoon dried sage
1 clove garlic, finely minced (½ teaspoon)
¼ cup dry white wine or vermouth
¼ cup chicken broth

Preheat oven to 350°. Place the chicken breasts on waxed paper and pound to about ¼-inch thickness. Place a slice of ham and one of cheese on each piece of chicken. Season with pepper, sage, and garlic. Roll up and fasten with toothpicks. Place in a greased baking dish and pour the wine and broth over them. Cover with foil. Bake 40 minutes. Chill. Cut into rounds. Serve on a platter with a tomato rose nestled in watercress in the center. *Makes 24.*

Can be frozen. Freeze the rolls and thaw overnight before cutting into rounds.

OLD-FASHIONED CHOPPED
CHICKEN LIVER

Since almost every Jewish grandmother made the best, this delicious spread needs no introduction. Recently all sorts of seasonings have been introduced, from tarragon or ginger to brandy or sherry to—perish the thought—crumbled bacon, but I still prefer the unadulterated version. For the real thing use a hand-held food chopper, not a blender or food processor.

    4 tablespoons chicken fat
    1 large Spanish onion, finely chopped (1¾ cups)
    4 cloves garlic, minced (2 teaspoons)
    ½ pound chicken livers
    1 teaspoon salt
    ¼ teaspoon freshly ground black pepper
    2 hard-cooked eggs, coarsely chopped

Melt the fat in a heavy skillet and sauté the onions for about 10 minutes. Add the garlic and sauté until the onions are golden. Meanwhile wash and clean the chicken livers and dry them thoroughly. Add the livers to the pan, raise the heat, and cook them quickly for about 4 to 5 minutes (they should still be slightly pink in the center). Add the salt and pepper and stir for another minute. Put the onions and livers in a wooden chopping bowl. Add the chopped eggs. With a hand-held food chopper, chop the mixture coarsely—you want a spread, but not a purée. Transfer the mixture to a bowl and cover with plastic wrap as the surface darkens quickly when exposed to the air. Serve with toasted cocktail-sized salty rye, melba toast, or any water cracker. *Makes about two cups.*

Note: Chicken fat is available in the dairy or meat cases of most supermarkets, but if you cannot obtain it, making your own is easy. It can also be used with excellent results for sautéing chicken or as a base for the ingredients of a poultry stuffing.

Cut 1 pound of chicken fat into small chunks. Place the fat and 2 large onions, finely minced, in a heavy saucepan and cook slowly over moderate heat until the fat has melted and the onions have turned brown. Remove from the heat and strain through cheesecloth into a jar. The rendered fat will keep about a month in the refrigerator.

PÂTÉS

Pâtés make an impressive addition to a cocktail party menu or a perfect main course for a lunch. A pâté encased in shimmering aspic makes a centerpiece so dazzlingly elegant that one often hesitates to cut into it. In spite of their legendary aura, pâtés are relatively easy to prepare at home. They can be made a week in advance and refrigerated until needed. (They may be frozen but the texture will deteriorate.) To make them really luxurious, place strips of ham, tongue, or veal between the layers of the ground-meat mixture. If you have just won the lottery, sliced or diced truffles make an elegant garnish. Pâtés can be baked in almost any kind of loaf pan; I use narrow rectangular terrines of enameled cast iron.

COUNTRY-STYLE PÂTÉ
(Pâté de Campagne, after Paul Carnevale)

The firm of P. Carnevale & Son (631 Ninth Avenue, New York, New York 10036) has been cited by eminent food authorities for its country-style pâté, sausages, and other delicacies. Through the years, Paul senior and I have become good friends, and this recipe is based on the one he uses to produce his *pâté de campagne* in 500-pound lots. After many tests and much tasting, I have whittled it down to average-household size. Like most pâtés, this one improves after being refrigerated a few days. This pâté fits into a 10- by 3¼- by 3-inch terrine, which holds 5 cups. The terrine must have a cover.

½ pound pork liver
2 pounds pork shoulder, not too lean
2 teaspoons salt
2 teaspoons dried thyme
¾ teaspoon freshly ground black pepper
¼ teaspoon freshly grated nutmeg
¼ teaspoon dried sage
8 cloves garlic, finely chopped
½ cup white wine
3 tablespoons lard
1 large onion, finely chopped (1½ cups)
1 bay leaf
2 eggs, beaten
¼ cup flour
½ cup shelled and skinned pistachio nuts
¾ pound sliced bacon

Cut the liver and meat into 1-inch pieces. Put into a large bowl and add the salt, thyme, pepper, nutmeg, sage, garlic, and ¼ cup of the wine. Using your hands (they are among the best utensils for making meat mixtures), turn the meats until they are coated with the marinade. Cover the bowl and marinate in the refrigerator overnight.

In a large skillet, melt the lard and sauté the onion in it with the bay leaf until the onion is golden. Add the remaining ¼ cup wine and cook until most of the wine has evaporated. Add the marinated meats to the skillet and sauté for about 5 minutes, stirring occasionally. Add the liver and continue to sauté until the surface of the meats has lost its red color. Cool for about 30 minutes. Put this mixture through the fine blade of a meat grinder or grind one-fourth of the mixture at a time in a food processor. When all has been ground, add the eggs, flour, and pistachio nuts.

Again using your hands, mix the ingredients until they are thoroughly amalgamated.

Preheat oven to 375°. Line the bottom and sides of a terrine with the bacon slices, overlapping the pieces and letting some hang over the sides. Pat the meat mixture in and overlap the bacon slices on the top; if necessary, add extra slices to cover the top surface completely. Place a double thickness of heavy foil securely over the terrine and then put on the cover. Put the terrine into a larger baking pan and pour in boiling water to reach halfway up the sides of the terrine. Bake 2 hours or until a meat thermometer inserted in the center registers 160°. Remove the terrine from the baking pan and pour off the water. Put the terrine back into the pan. Remove the cover but leave the foil intact. Weigh the foil down with some heavy cans or a brick. This weighting squeezes out the excess fat and compresses the pâté for proper texture and easier slicing. Let the pâté sit at room temperature for about 4 hours. Put another double thickness of foil under the bottom of the terrine, extending it a little way up the sides. Refrigerate it, with the weights still on, at least overnight.

The pâté may be served directly from the terrine. However, the bacon, although thoroughly cooked, may look distastefully raw to many people, so I prefer to turn the pâté out of the terrine and peel off the bacon. Run a sharp knife inside along the edges of the terrine, then put it in about 1 inch of very hot water for 1 minute. Invert it over a piece of foil. With a sharp knife, carefully peel off the bacon. Turn the loaf right side up on a serving dish, slice, and serve. Or wrap it securely in foil and refrigerate.

QUICK ASPIC FOR PÂTÉ

For a really festive appearance, enclose the pâté in this aspic, which is quick but delicious.

2 envelopes gelatin
⅔ cup Madeira
2 10½-ounce cans consommé with gelatin

Dissolve the gelatin in the wine. Heat the consommé with the gelatin, stirring until it is dissolved. Cool until it just begins to get syrupy. Meanwhile, remove the pâté from its pan, wash and dry the pan, and pour about ½ inch of the aspic into it. Let the aspic set in the refrigerator. Make flower-shaped cutouts of carrots and hard-cooked egg whites with truffle cutters, using scallion tops for stems. When the aspic in the terrine is set, dip the decorations in the remaining unset aspic and place them on the set aspic in the bottom of the terrine. Pour over another layer of aspic and refrigerate again. When this has set, carefully place the pâté on the set aspic (you may have to trim the edges of the pâté to make room for the aspic). Pour the rest of the aspic in around the sides of the pâté. Refrigerate at least overnight but not more than 2 days. When ready to serve, unmold on a platter. An easier way to use the aspic is to pour it into a large baking pan and refrigerate until set, then cut it into diamonds or cubes and surround the unmolded pâté with these. *Makes 3 cups aspic.*

CHICKEN-LIVER PÂTÉ

This pâté is much quicker and easier to make than the preceding one but the result is still impressive. The use of ready-made sausage meat eliminates the need for a meat grinder or food processor; the livers are quickly puréed in a blender. Only the garnishes are marinated and these for only half an hour. The spice mixture can be prepared in large quantities and kept tightly sealed to use as needed. This pâté fits into a 10- by 3¼ - by 3-inch terrine, which holds 5 cups.

SPICE MIXTURE
¼ teaspoon ground ginger
¼ teaspoon freshly grated nutmeg
¼ teaspoon ground cloves
½ teaspoon freshly ground pepper

PÂTÉ MIXTURE
⅛-pound slice ham and ⅛-pound slice smoked tongue,
    both sliced ⅜-inch thick, ⅜-inch wide

¾ cup Madeira
¾ teaspoon spice mixture
1 tablespoon butter
½ cup finely chopped onions
1¼ pound chicken livers
1 pound pork sausage meat
2 cloves garlic, put through garlic press (1 teaspoon)
1½ teaspoons salt
½ cup shelled and skinned pistachio nuts
2 eggs, beaten
¾ pound sliced bacon
½ teaspoon crumbled dried thyme
1 bay leaf

Put the ham and tongue strips into a small bowl. Combine ¼ cup of the Madeira and ¼ teaspoon of the spice mixture and pour over the meat. Let marinate while preparing the pâté. Melt the butter in a small skillet and sauté the onion until golden. Add the remaining ½ cup Madeira and cook until most of the liquid has evaporated. Put the chicken livers into a blender or food processor and purée them. Put the sausage meat into a large bowl. Add the chicken livers, garlic, salt, the remaining ½ teaspoon spice mixture, the nuts, and the eggs. Combine thoroughly.

Preheat oven to 375°. Drain the marinated meat slices. Line the bottom and sides of the terrine with the bacon slices, overlapping the pieces and letting some hang over the sides. Pour in half the sausage–chicken liver mixture. Cover with the meat slices, arranged lengthwise in a decorative pattern. Add the rest of the sausage mixture. Sprinkle the top with the crumbled, dried thyme and put the bay leaf in the center. Overlap the bacon slices over the top and continue as in the preceding recipe. *Makes 25 to 30 slices.*

EDNA'S JIFFY CHICKEN-LIVER PÂTÉ IN ASPIC

This deliciously spiced, smooth pâté under a glistening golden, green-flecked aspic is deceptively simple to make.

1 13¾-ounce can chicken broth
1 envelope gelatin
¼ cup finely chopped curly parsley
1 pound chicken livers
½ pound butter plus 4 tablespoons, at room temperature
1 tablespoon plus 2 teaspoons brandy
½ cup finely chopped onions
1 teaspoon salt
¼ teaspoon freshly ground black pepper
¼ teaspoon ground cloves
¼ teaspoon freshly ground nutmeg
parsley
ripe olives

Chill the broth in the refrigerator for an hour before opening. Remove any fat that may be on the surface. Place the broth and the gelatin in a saucepan and heat until the gelatin has dissolved. Add the parsley and stir to distribute it. Pour into a shallow 9-inch mold (a layer-cake pan is perfect for this). Chill in the refrigerator until firm, about ½ hour. Meanwhile rinse and clean the chicken livers. Dry them thoroughly on paper towels. In a large skillet, heat the 4 tablespoons butter. Add the livers and sauté them over medium-high heat until they are well browned but still pink in the center, usually about 10 minutes. Put the livers into the container of an electric blender or a food processor. Deglaze the skillet with the 2 teaspoons of brandy. Pour the scrapings into the container with the livers. Cut the remaining ½ pound butter into cubes and add, along with the remaining 1 tablespoon brandy, the onion, salt, pepper, cloves, and nutmeg. Run the motor until you have a smooth purée. Pour the mixture over the set gelatin. Cover with plastic wrap and refrigerate for at least 4 hours or up to 2 days. When ready to serve, unmold on a plate and surround with parsley. Decorate the top surface with slices of pitted ripe olives. *Makes 16 to 20 servings.*

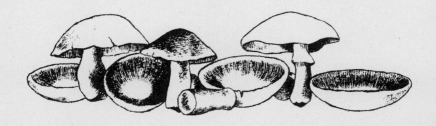

EVERYMAN'S PÂTÉ ·

This pâté can hold its own with most tinned French pâtés and is a great deal cheaper. All the ingredients are readily available and can be assembled quickly.

½ pound good-quality braunschweiger
2 tablespoons butter, softened to room temperature
2 teaspoons grated onion
1 teaspoon prepared mustard, preferably German
1 tablespoon cognac
2 dashes Tabasco
¼ teaspoon dried tarragon
1 clove garlic, put through press (¼ teaspoon)
1 teaspoon Worcestershire sauce
¼ teaspoon salt
2 tablespoons Duxelles (see index)
4 tablespoons finely chopped parsley or
    chopped unsalted shelled pistachio nuts

Combine all the ingredients, except the parsley or pistachio nuts, in the bowl of an electric mixer or a food processor. Process until well blended. Refrigerate the mixture several hours or overnight. Serve as a spread with chopped parsley sprinkled on top, or form into 1-inch balls and roll in chopped parsley or pistachio nuts, or use as a filling for turnover rolls, scooped-out French bread or rolls, or brioche.

To make it into a mold, line a 1-cup bowl with plastic wrap, leaving enough to cover the top. Put the mixture in, cover with the additional plastic wrap, and refrigerate overnight. Lift out the wrap, place the mold on a plate, and peel off the wrap. Decorate with chopped parsley or pistachio nuts. *Makes 1 cup.*

Cold
Cheese Hors d'Oeuvres

Now that American taste buds have been educated to appreciate foods from all over the world, there are few people who do not relish some variety of cheese. To assure freshness, try to purchase cheeses at a store that specializes in them. Served with crusty bread or plain crackers, they are an easy and deservedly popular choice. To be at its best, cheese should always be served at room temperature. At most wine tastings, cheese is the only food served to "cleanse the palate" between samplings. More and more people are using the wine-tasting theme for an innovative and easy-to-assemble cocktail party. However, cheese can also be the basis for many appetizers. In addition to spreads and balls or rolls, cheeses can be transformed into interesting molds.

UNBAKED CHEESE FINGERS

An easy and unusual way to serve cheese. Well-wrapped in foil, these will keep in the refrigerator for days.

     1 pound Brie cheese
     4 tablespoons butter
     2 teaspoons dry mustard
     6 slices Swiss cheese (about ½ pound), cut into slices
          7 inches long, 3½ inches wide, and ⅛ inch thick

Cut the rind off the Brie (unfortunately, you will have only about ½ pound left). Let the Brie and the butter soften to room temperature, and put them in a medium-sized bowl. Add the mustard and stir all together until you have a homogenized mixture. Put a slice of the Swiss cheese on a piece of foil and spread it with part of the mixture. Cover with a second slice, and spread that with more of the mixture; then cover with a third slice to make a triple-decker sandwich. Wrap securely in the foil, and press down lightly. Repeat with the remaining ingredients. When ready to serve, cut each sandwich into fingers about 1¾ inches long and ¾ inch wide. Put a decorative toothpick into each. Cherry tomatoes on a bed of watercress make an attractive center for the platter. *Makes 40 fingers.*

Can be frozen. Thaw overnight in the refrigerator.

MOLLY'S BRIE IN A CRUST
(Brie en Croûte)

1 8- or 9-inch frozen pie shell, thawed
1 4½-ounce can Brie
1 egg beaten with 1 tablespoon heavy cream

Preheat oven to 350°. When the pie shell has thawed sufficiently to be pliable, cut off the fluted rim and the sides, leaving a flat circle of dough. Place the Brie in the center of the pastry and gently ease the crust, a quarter section at a time, around it until the cheese is covered. As you work, brush each edge with the egg-cream wash to seal the edges. Place the pastry-covered cheese on a baking sheet. Brush the entire surface with more of the egg-cream wash. With a sharp knife, pierce a hole in the center of the crust. (You can cut decorative leaves from the leftover scraps of dough, place them on the top, and brush them with the egg-cream wash.) Bake 35 minutes. You can prepare this a few hours ahead but do not give it the final egg-cream wash until just before baking. *Makes 6 servings.*

STUFFED GOUDA CHEESE

2 tablespoons sesame seeds
1 10-ounce round imported Gouda cheese
¼ cup Heineken lager beer
2 tablespoons butter
1 teaspoon German mustard
1 teaspoon Worcestershire sauce
½ teaspoon celery salt
1 teaspoon chopped chives
¼ teaspoon salt
2 dashes Tabasco

Preheat oven to 350°. Place the sesame seeds on a cookie sheet and bake 5 minutes. Remove and cool. Cut a 2¼-inch circle from the top of the Gouda cheese. Set the lid aside. With a sharp, curved knife, preferably a grapefruit knife, carefully remove the cheese from the outer coating. Once the bulk of the cheese is removed, use a teaspoon to remove the remainder, working carefully to avoid puncturing the shell. Cut the cheese into small dice, and grate coarsely in a blender or food processor, or with a hand grater. Put the grated cheese into the bowl of an electric blender or food processor. Add the remaining ingredients, folding in the sesame seeds. Carefully fill the shell with the mixture, reserving any excess to refill when necessary. Replace the top of the cheese and wrap the ball in plastic wrap. Chill overnight. Serve surrounded with pumpernickel squares or Swedish or Finnish flatbread. *Makes ¾ cup.*

ROQUEFORT BRANDY SPREAD

This easy mixture makes a delicious stuffing for vegetables or can be served with raw vegetables or melba toast. It will keep for weeks in the refrigerator. You can substitute blue cheese, but the result will not be as subtle.

1 pound Roquefort cheese
½ pound cream cheese
3 tablespoons butter
¼ teaspoon dry mustard
pinch cayenne pepper
¼ cup cognac

Put all the ingredients in an electric blender or food processor and let soften to room temperature. Purée or beat until you have a homogenous mixture. Transfer to a bowl, cover tightly, and refrigerate. *Makes 2½ cups.*

GORGONZOLA SPREAD

½ pound Gorgonzola, at room temperature
¼ pound butter, at room temperature
6 dashes Tabasco
½ cup dry vermouth
6 tablespoons chopped roasted almonds

Put the Gorgonzola and butter in the bowl of an electric blender or food processor. Blend until smooth. Add the Tabasco and vermouth and blend until they are incorporated. Remove the mixture to a bowl and fold in the almonds. Use to stuff celery or endive stalks or mushrooms, or serve with crackers or melba toast. *Makes about 1 cup.*

ENGLISH WALNUT SPREAD

Mash 8 ounces Gorgonzola with 8 ounces cream cheese until thoroughly combined. Drain and mash 8 pickled walnuts (Escoffier or Crosse & Blackwell), add, and stir until completely incorporated. Chill. *Makes about 2½ cups.*

Can be frozen. Thaw overnight in the refrigerator.

ITALIAN PORCUPINE SPREAD

¼ pound whipped cream cheese
½ pound prosciutto, finely minced
3 tablespoons finely chopped Italian parsley
1 tablespoon finely chopped chives
½ teaspoon freshly ground black pepper
¼ cup sour cream
Italian bread sticks

Combine all ingredients except the bread sticks. Put in serving bowl. Break the bread sticks into 3-inch pieces and stick them into the surface. The mixture can also be used for filling Profiteroles (see index). *Makes about 1 cup.*

GREEK SALAD SPREAD

Feta cheese and the other tangy ingredients of Greek Salad can be incorporated into a sprightly spread.

½ pound feta cheese
1 small cucumber, peeled, seeded, and
   coarsely chopped (¼ cup)
4 tablespoons finely chopped dill
3 tablespoons chopped Calamata olives
2 tablespoons chopped scallions
6 grinds black pepper
2 tablespoons yogurt

Drain the feta cheese on paper towels. Place it in a bowl and break it up. Add the rest of the ingredients and stir to blend well. Taste for salt (usually the feta cheese has enough). Cover and chill several hours or overnight. *Makes about 1½ cups.*

FRENCH GARLIC HERB CHEESE

½ pound French cream cheese, such as Rondolé,
  or Philadelphia cream cheese
½ teaspoon dried thyme
½ teaspoon dried chervil
½ teaspoon dried summer savory
2 tablespoons lemon juice
½ teaspoon freshly ground black pepper
1 clove garlic, put through press

Let the cheese soften to room temperature. With a mortar and pestle, pulverize the dried herbs and then soak them for 10 minutes in the lemon juice. Beat the cheese until smooth. Add the herbs, lemon juice, pepper, and garlic and beat until homogenized. Cover and chill. This mixture can be used as a spread, or to make Bologna Frisbies (see index). *Makes about 1¼ cups.*

FENNEL–BEL PAESE BALLS

With so many commercial versions of Cheddar cheese balls and rolls available, why not try other varieties of cheeses? Although tiny cheese balls require a little more work than the tennis-ball size, I find them more attractive and easier to serve—no utensils or plates are required.

½ pound Bel Paese cheese
½ cup fresh fennel sprigs, finely chopped
2 teaspoons onion juice
1 teaspoon anchovy paste
⅔ cup pine nuts

Remove the rind from the cheese. Let soften in a bowl to room temperature. Add the fennel, onion juice, and anchovy paste and mix to combine. Cover and chill. Preheat oven to 350°. Place the pine nuts on an ungreased baking sheet. Toast 7–8 minutes, shaking the pan twice. Watch carefully, as they burn easily. Remove to paper towels to cool. Place the nuts on a sheet of waxed paper. With a measuring teaspoon, form the cheese mixture into balls, using your palms to smooth and round them. Roll each ball in the nuts until it is covered. Place the balls on a serving dish, cover with plastic wrap, and chill for a few hours or overnight. *Makes 12.*

ROQUEFORT-ALMOND BALLS

¼ pound Roquefort cheese
¼ pound cream cheese
1 tablespoon cognac
2 dashes Tabasco
¾ cup chopped toasted almonds
1 tablespoon finely chopped chives

Let cheeses soften to room temperature. Cream in an electric blender or food processor. Beat in the cognac and Tabasco. Stir in ¼ cup of the almonds and the chives. Chill for a few hours or overnight. Form into 1-inch balls and roll in the remaining ½ cup almonds. This mixture can also be used to fill Stuffed Ham Rolls (see index). *Makes 16 balls.*

CHEESE ROLL OR CHEESE BALLS
WITH PECANS

4 ounces Liederkranz cheese
4 ounces Taleggio cheese
4 ounces aged Gouda cheese
2 tablespoons Madeira
¾ cup coarsely chopped pecans

Place the Liederkranz and Taleggio in the bowl of an electric blender or food processor. Let soften to room temperature. Grate the Gouda cheese. Mix all the cheeses in the blender or food processor. Gradually mix in the Madeira. Place the cheese mixture on a piece of plastic wrap and shape into a roll approximately 10 by 1½ inches. Chill overnight. Finish shaping the roll when it is cold. Place the chopped pecans on a sheet of waxed paper and roll the cheese mixture in it until all the surfaces are covered with pecans. Rewrap the roll in plastic wrap and chill for a few hours or up to 2 days.

To make balls: with a measuring teaspoon form the chilled mixture into balls about 1 inch in diameter, and roll each in the pecans. *Makes one 10-inch by 1½-inch roll or about 21 balls.*

CHEESE AND WALNUT ROLL

5 ounces Kraft Sharp Old English Cheese
¼ pound blue cheese
1 3-ounce package cream cheese with chives
¼ cup tawny port wine
1 teaspoon onion juice
⅛ teaspoon chili powder
1½ cups coarsely chopped black walnuts

Put the three cheeses into the bowl of an electric mixer or a food processor, and let soften to room temperature. Add the wine, onion juice, and chili powder. Blend well. Fold in ½ cup of the walnuts. Place the mixture on waxed paper and roll it into a log about 10 inches long and 1¼ inches wide. Wrap in plastic wrap and chill for at least 4 hours or overnight. Spread the remaining 1 cup walnuts on a sheet of waxed paper and roll the cheese log back and forth on the nuts until the entire surface is coated. Rewrap in plastic wrap and chill again. To serve, place on a long platter or board and let the guests cut slices to put on crisp crackers or cocktail pumpernickel. *Makes one 10-inch by 1½-inch roll, about 20 slices.*

SAP SAGO ROLL

½ pound cream cheese, softened to room temperature
6 tablespoons grated Sap Sago cheese
½ cup grated Gruyère cheese (⅛ pound)
½ cup toasted salted pistachio nuts

In the bowl of an electric mixer, combine all the cheeses. On waxed paper, form the mixture into a roll measuring about 8 by 1¼ inches. Wrap securely in the waxed paper. Chill for a few hours or overnight. Place the nuts on a sheet of waxed paper. Remove the waxed paper from the cheese roll and rotate the roll gently over the nuts until it is coated. Rewrap securely in waxed paper and chill for a few hours or several days. Serve with pumpernickel squares. *Makes 16 to 24 slices.*
Can be frozen. Thaw roll overnight in refrigerator.

GORGONZOLA PROSCIUTTO ROLLS

1 pound Gorgonzola cheese
¼ pound cream cheese
¼ cup dry cocktail sherry
¼ pound prosciutto, finely chopped (⅔ cup)

Let the cheeses soften to room temperature. Use an electric mixer, a food processor, or a wooden spoon to combine cheeses. Gradually stir in the sherry and beat until well mixed. Place half of the cheese mixture on waxed paper, and form a roll about 8 inches long and 1½ inches wide. Roll the other half of the mixture in the same fashion. Chill a few hours or overnight. When the rolls are firm, sprinkle ⅓ cup of the prosciutto on waxed paper and place one cheese roll on it. Pat the prosciutto around the roll until it is completely covered. Repeat with the other half of the cheese mixture. Refrigerate rolls again. Serve with small slices of Italian bread. *Makes 32 to 48 slices.*

PARMESAN CHEESE MOLD
(Il Duomo)

A cheese mold is an attractive addition to the cocktail table and a boon to the hostess, as it can be prepared two days in advance and requires a minimum of work.

1 cup beef consommé with gelatin
1 envelope gelatin
1 teaspoon Italian herb seasoning
3 ounces cream cheese, softened to room temperature
½ cup grated Parmesan cheese
¼ pound finely ground ham
1 teaspoon dry mustard
¼ cup chopped chives
2 tablespoons chopped ripe olives

GARNISH
cherry tomato halves
sprigs of curly parsley
slices of black olives

Put the consommé into a small saucepan and sprinkle the gelatin over it. Heat until the gelatin is dissolved. Stir in the herb seasoning. Put into a bowl and chill until syrupy. Blend in the cream cheese, Parmesan cheese, ham, and mustard. Fold in the chives and olives. Oil a mold with vegetable oil, or spray with nonstick vegetable cooking spray. Pour in the cheese mixture and chill for 4 hours or overnight. When ready to serve, unmold on a plate and surround the base with cherry tomato halves and sprigs of curly parsley. Decorate the top with the olive slices. Serve with wheat crackers. *Fills a 1½-cup mold.*

CAMEMBERT-KIRSCH-ALMOND MOLD

8 ounces Camembert cheese
4 ounces Liederkranz cheese
3 tablespoons Kirschwasser
4 ounces cream cheese
1 teaspoon Worcestershire sauce
½ teaspoon celery seed
¼ cup coarsely chopped toasted almonds

Remove the rinds from the Camembert and Liederkranz. Place in a small bowl and cover with the Kirschwasser. Cover with plastic wrap and let stand at room temperature for 1 hour. Drain the cheeses, reserving the Kirschwasser, and place them with the cream cheese in the bowl of an electric mixer or food processor. Beat until well blended, then gradually beat in the reserved Kirschwasser, the Worcestershire sauce, and the celery seed. Fold in the almonds. Line a 1½- or 1¼-cup soufflé dish with plastic wrap, leaving enough overlap to cover the top. Pat the cheese mixture into the mold. Cover the top with the extra plastic wrap. Refrigerate 6 hours or overnight. To unmold, remove the plastic wrap and place on a serving dish. Decorate the top, if desired, with halves of toasted almonds. *Makes 1¼ cups.*

TRIPART CHEESE MOLD

4 ounces Liederkranz cheese, chilled
½ pound well-aged Cheddar, grated
2 ounces blue cheese, crumbled
2 ounces cream cheese
½ cup imported dark beer
2 teaspoons juice of grated onion
½ teaspoon Dijon mustard
1 teaspoon Escoffier Sauce Diable
1 teaspoon celery salt
½ teaspoon salt
1 teaspoon Worcestershire sauce
dash cayenne pepper
2 cloves garlic, crushed (1 teaspoon)

Remove the rind from the Liederkranz while it is still chilled. Place the Liederkranz, Cheddar, blue cheese, and cream cheese in the bowl of an electric mixer or food processor. Let stand about ½ hour to soften to room temperature. Cream the cheeses together, gradually adding the beer. When all is well blended, add the remaining ingredients. Beat again until all the seasonings are incorporated. Line a 2-cup soufflé dish with plastic wrap, leaving enough overlap to cover the top. Pat the cheese mixture into the dish. Cover the top with plastic wrap and refrigerate at least 6 hours or preferably overnight. To unmold, remove from the mold and peel off the wrap. *Makes 2 cups.*

Hot
Hors d'Oeuvres

Hot
Vegetables

With the increasing number of vegetarians, hostesses preparing a party often need to keep their food restrictions in mind. However, vegetables, properly cooked and seasoned, will appeal even to those whose tastes run chiefly to steak and chocolate cake.

FOO YUNG D'OEUVRES

½ cup bean sprouts, preferably fresh
¼ cup Chinese dried mushrooms
1 cup crabmeat, fresh or canned
2 tablespoons finely minced scallions
2 tablespoons finely minced celery
2 tablespoons finely minced water chestnuts
1 teaspoon dry sherry
1 tablespoon soy sauce
1 clove garlic, minced (½ teaspoon)
¾ teaspoon grated fresh ginger
¼ teaspoon monosodium glutamate (optional)
pinch sugar
pinch freshly ground black pepper
½ cup cornstarch
3 eggs, beaten
peanut oil for frying

Rinse and drain bean sprouts. If you are using canned bean sprouts, open the can a few hours ahead of time, drain the sprouts, place in a strainer, and run cold water over them. Place drained sprouts in a bowl with cold water to cover and refrigerate a few hours. Wash the mushrooms, place in a bowl, cover with hot water, and soak half an hour. Drain and squeeze dry. Cut off the tough stems and discard. Mince the caps. Drain the bean sprouts thoroughly and dry them on paper towels. Combine all ingredients except the peanut oil (include monosodium glutamate if used). Stir the mixture with a large fork until ingredients are thoroughly combined.

Pour peanut oil into a medium-sized saucepan or electric skillet to a depth of 1½ inches and heat to 400°. Using a ½ teaspoon measuring spoon, drop a few spoonfuls of the mixture at a time into the hot fat. They should rise and be brown in about 1 minute. Turn and cook another minute. Line a jelly-roll pan with paper towels and with a slotted spoon remove cooked patties to the pan. Keep them warm in a 200° oven. Continue until all the batter is used. Recheck the temperature of the oil every few minutes.

Place a cocktail pick in each patty. (Chinese fortune picks add an appropriate touch.) Serve Duck Sauce or Orange-Soy Dip (see index) in the center of the platter. Scatter scallion brushes among the patties.

These can be made in advance and reheated in a 400° oven for 8 minutes. *Makes 50.*

Can be frozen. Freeze in foil trays and secure tightly in plastic bags. While still frozen, heat in a 400° oven for 10 to 12 minutes, or until piping hot.

ERNIE'S MINIATURE STUFFED CABBAGE ROLLS

Almost every European country has its version of stuffed cabbage —the French even make it into a gala presentation by stuffing a whole cabbage and presenting it so the finished dish resembles a huge vegetable *bombe*. These miniatures are ideal for a cocktail hors d'oeuvre to be kept hot in a chafing dish. They may be made two days in advance, but, even better, they freeze very well.

SAUCE
1 29-ounce can tomatoes
4 cups tomato juice
juice of 2 lemons (½ cup)
1½ cups brown sugar
2 cups finely diced onions

1 large green cabbage, about 2½ pounds
1 pound ground round beef
¼ cup raw rice
2 teaspoons salt
¼ teaspoon freshly ground black pepper
½ cup raisins

Drain the tomatoes, reserving the juice. Chop the pulp and put it and the reserved juice in a large heavy saucepan. Add the 4 cups tomato juice, the lemon juice, brown sugar, and onion. Bring to a boil and stir to combine ingredients. Lower heat to a simmer. Meanwhile trim and core the cabbage. Drop it into a large pot filled with lightly salted boiling water. Boil for 8 to 10 minutes, or until the leaves are pliable. Drain the cabbage in a colander and run cold water over the leaves. When the cabbage is cool enough to handle, carefully place each leaf on paper towels and pat dry. Cut each leaf in half along the tough center stem, removing the stem as you cut. Place the half leaves, curved side down, on the working surface with the wide side toward you. In a bowl combine the beef, rice, salt, pepper, and 6 tablespoons of the simmering sauce. Add the raisins to the remaining sauce and continue simmering. Place about 1 teaspoon of the meat filling on the edge of a half leaf. Roll it once away from you, then tuck in the two sides, and continue to roll away from you until the mixture is enclosed and the leaf is formed into a tight, fat, cigar-shaped package. Place each roll as filled on a large tray seam side down. When all are completed, place them seam side down in the simmering sauce. Simmer, covered, for 1 hour, basting every 15 minutes, then uncover the pot and simmer another ½ hour. *Makes about 60.*

Can be frozen. Freeze in sauce in a freezer container. Thaw overnight in the refrigerator and reheat, covered, slowly.

EGGPLANT TRIANGLES

One summer when our garden surprised us with an oversupply of eggplant, I used Beer Batter (see index) to create these bite-sized hors d'oeuvres, which have been an all-star winner.

> 1 ¾-pound eggplant
> ½ cup flour
> ½ teaspoon salt
> 1 recipe Beer Batter (see index)
> oil for deep frying
> salt and pepper (optional)

Slice off both ends of the eggplant. Do not peel. Cut across into ¼-inch slices. Cut each slice into quarters. Combine the flour and ½ teaspoon salt in a plastic bag. Heat the oil in a deep-fryer to 375.° Shake the eggplant triangles in the bag until coated. Add 1 tablespoon of the hot oil to the Beer Batter and stir. Dip the flour-coated eggplant slices into the batter and fry in the deep-fryer a few at a time, about 2 minutes a side. Remove with a spatula. Drain on paper towels, and place on paper towels in a 200° oven to keep warm until all the pieces have been fried. Sprinkle the slices with salt and pepper or serve with Chinese Fish Sauce, Tartare Sauce, Homemade Duck Sauce (see index) or, if you can obtain Chinese sesame-seed paste (not the same as Middle Eastern *tahini*), try the dip in the following recipe.

To reheat, place a rack on a jelly-roll pan. Put the eggplant triangles on the rack and heat in a preheated 425° oven for 5 minutes. *Makes about 50.*

Can be frozen. Freeze on a flat surface and then put into plastic freezer bags and seal. Reheat, frozen, as above, but heat for 10 minutes.

ZUCCHINI STRIPS

In one of our favorite Italian restaurants a bowl of tiny fried zucchini strips appears on the table as soon as you sit down. Theirs are merely tossed in seasoned flour and deep fried, but I prefer to use Beer Batter. Cut small zucchini in matchlike strips and toss them with some salt in a bowl. Let them sit for half an hour, then wash off the salt and dry them thoroughly. Prepare as in main recipe. Serve these with just a sprinkling of salt.

SESAME-SEED DIP

½ cup sour cream
10 teaspoons Chinese sesame-seed paste
6 dashes Tabasco
4 teaspoons dark soy sauce

Combine all ingredients.

SILVER-DOLLAR POTATO PANCAKES

Although potato pancakes are usually associated with pot roast and bowls of cinnamony applesauce, they can be a rather unusual accompaniment to cocktails. In that setting, they are better served with a bowl of sour cream, sprinkled with chopped chives or parsley, or, if you have just received an income-tax refund, serve with caviar and chopped onion. A food processor will eliminate the tedious grating. If you can obtain Potato White (made by Topline Foods Corp., Jersey City, New Jersey 07302 and available in specialty stores), you do not have to work nonstop to prevent the potatoes from darkening.

About 6 medium-sized baking potatoes
  (1½ cups, well packed, after grating)
1 teaspoon Potato White
2 eggs, slightly beaten
¼ cup finely grated onion
1½ tablespoons flour
1 teaspoon baking powder
1½ teaspoons salt
½ teaspoon freshly ground black pepper
5 tablespoons butter
6 tablespoons vegetable oil

Peel the potatoes and drop them into a bowl of cold water. When all are peeled, dry them with paper towels. Grate them in a food processor or on the fine side of a grater. Dissolve the Potato White in a bowl of cold water. Squeeze the grated potatoes by handfuls and put them into a measuring cup. When you have 1½ cups, well packed, drop them into the cold water. If you do not have Potato White, immediately put the grated potatoes in the cold water. Soak them for 5 minutes, squeeze them again, and refrigerate them covered for a few hours if desired. Add the beaten eggs, grated onion, flour, baking powder, salt, and pepper. Beat the mixture with a fork until thoroughly combined. Preheat oven to 250°. Line jelly-roll pans with paper towels. Put 2½ tablespoons of the butter and 3 tablespoons of the oil in a large skillet and heat until the butter stops foaming. Then drop in the potato mixture by half-teaspoons, about 10 at a time. Press each down with a small spatula. Fry for about 3 minutes a side or until the bottom is golden. Turn each with a spatula and fry until other side is golden. Put on the towel-lined jelly-roll pans and set pans in the oven. Heat the remaining butter and oil and fry the rest of the potato mixture. If necessary, add a bit more butter and oil. These will stay crisp for about 10 minutes in the oven.

You may make them a day in advance. To reheat, place on a wire rack set on a jelly-roll pan. Bake 5 minutes in a preheated 400° oven. *Makes about 36.*

Can be frozen. Freeze on a flat surface, then place in layers with foil between. Seal in bags. To serve, place frozen pancakes on rack as above and reheat for 7 minutes in a preheated 425° oven.

STUFFED MUSHROOMS

MUSHROOMS ROMA

12 large mushrooms, about 1½ inches in diameter
11 tablespoons butter

1 clove garlic, crushed
½ cup finely minced onion
1 clove garlic, minced
4 Italian sweet sausages (½ pound)
2 tablespoons chopped parsley
4 tablespoons fine bread crumbs
1 egg, beaten
½ teaspoon dried basil
¼ teaspoon dried tarragon
½ teaspoon dried oregano
2 tablespoons pine nuts
3 tablespoons dry sherry
5 tablespoons grated Parmesan cheese
salt

Preheat oven to 350°. Wipe the mushrooms with a damp towel and gently ease the stems off. Mince the stems fine and reserve. Melt 7 tablespoons of the butter in a large skillet, add the garlic, and cook 2 minutes. Remove the pan from the fire. Dip the mushroom caps into the melted butter until well coated on all sides. Grease a jelly-roll pan or baking dish with 1 tablespoon butter, put in the mushrooms, cap side down, and reserve. Sauté the minced onion in 2 tablespoons of the remaining butter in a skillet until translucent. Add the minced mushroom stems and the garlic and sauté another 5 minutes. Remove the sausages from their casings, then break up the sausages and sauté them in another skillet until cooked through, pouring off the fat as it accumulates. Remove them with a slotted spoon. Combine with the minced onion, mushroom stems, garlic mixture, parsley, bread crumbs, egg, basil, tarragon, oregano, pine nuts, 1 tablespoon of the sherry, and 1 tablespoon of the grated Parmesan cheese. Taste and add salt if needed. Pile the mixture into the mushroom caps. Sprinkle with the remaining 4 tablespoons grated Parmesan, and use the remaining tablespoon butter to dot each cap. Put back in baking pan and add the remaining 2 tablespoons sherry to the pan. Bake 20 to 25 minutes. Baste two or three times while baking. These can be served warm in a chafing dish. *Makes 12.*

Can be frozen. Freeze on a foil baking tray. Thaw overnight

in refrigerator. Just before baking, grease baking pan, put in mushrooms cap side down, and add 2 additional tablespoons sherry to baking pan. Bake as directed above.

PROSCIUTTO-STUFFED MUSHROOMS

16 large mushrooms, about 2 inches in diameter
½ pound butter
2 cloves garlic, put through the press (½ teaspoon)
¼ cup chopped shallots
¾ pound prosciutto, finely chopped
1 cup fresh basil, finely chopped, or 6 tablespoons dried
¾ cup fine dry bread crumbs
6 tablespoons pine nuts
6 tablespoons finely grated Parmesan cheese
½ teaspoon freshly ground black pepper
¼ cup dry Marsala
2 eggs, beaten
4 tablespoons butter, melted

Preheat oven to 350°. Wipe the mushrooms with a damp towel and gently ease the stems off and reserve stems. In a large heavy skillet melt the ½ pound butter, add the garlic, and cook for 2 minutes. Remove the pan from the fire. Dip each cap in the garlic butter, making sure that the entire cap is covered. With a pastry brush, butter the baking dish with the remaining 2 tablespoons melted butter. Place mushrooms, cap side down, in baking dish. Reserve the butter. Chop the mushroom stems fine. In the garlic butter, sauté the mushroom stems and the shallots for 10 minutes. Add the prosciutto and basil, and sauté 2 minutes more. Remove to a large bowl. Add the bread crumbs, pine nuts, 2 tablespoons of the Parmesan cheese, the parsley, pepper, and beaten eggs. Mix well. Pile the mixture into the mushroom caps, mounding it slightly in the center. Sprinkle the caps with the remaining Parmesan cheese and 2 tablespoons of the melted butter. Bake for 20 minutes.

If mushrooms are not to be served immediately, place them

in a chafing dish or on a hot tray. Provide forks and plates. *Makes 16.*

Can be frozen. Follow directions for Mushrooms Roma, omitting sherry.

MUSHROOMS TARTARE

24 large mushrooms, about 2 inches in diameter
6 tablespoons butter
2 cloves garlic, crushed
1 pound ground round beef
¼ cup onion juice
2 cloves garlic, put through garlic press (½ teaspoon)
1 teaspoon salt
¼ teaspoon freshly ground black pepper
1 teaspoon Worcestershire sauce
½ teaspoon Dijon mustard
1 egg, beaten
catchup

Preheat oven to 350°. Wipe the mushrooms with a damp towel and gently ease the stems off. (Reserve stems for other use.) In a large heavy oven-proof skillet melt 4 tablespoons of the butter, add the 2 cloves garlic, and cook for 2 minutes. Remove the skillet from the heat. Dip each mushroom cap in the garlic butter, making sure that the entire cap is covered. Turn over to drain and return to skillet, cap side down. Remove the garlic, add the remaining 2 tablespoons butter, and bake in 350° oven for 10 minutes. Place on dish suitable for broiling. In a large bowl, combine the ground beef, onion juice, 1 clove crushed garlic, salt, pepper, Worcestershire sauce, Dijon mustard, and beaten egg. Pile the mixture in the prepared mushroom caps, mounding it slightly in the center. With a ¼ teaspoon measure, make an indentation in the center of the meat in each cap. Broil 3 minutes. Remove and place a dot of catchup in each indentation. (It may be necessary to press the indentation again.)

If mushrooms are not to be served immediately, place in a

chafing dish or on a hot tray. They may also be served on toasted rye bread rounds, cut to fit the mushroom caps. *Makes 24.*

Can be frozen. Freeze before broiling. Thaw in refrigerator overnight. Broil and dot with catchup as above.

CHRISTMAS MUSHROOMS FOR VEGETARIANS

8 tablespoons butter (¼ pound)
12 large mushrooms, about 2 inches in diameter
4 cloves garlic, finely chopped (2 teaspoons)
¼ cup finely chopped onion
6 tablespoons finely chopped green pepper
6 tablespoons finely chopped pimiento
¼ cup fine dry bread crumbs
1 egg, beaten
½ teaspoon salt
¼ teaspoon freshly ground black pepper
4 teaspoons minced parsley
1 teaspoon dried basil
½ teaspoon dried oregano

Preheat oven to 350°. Put 5 tablespoons of the butter in a jelly-roll pan and place in the oven for butter to melt. Wipe the mushrooms with a damp towel and gently ease the stems off. Chop the stems fine and reserve. When the butter is melted, remove pan from the oven and roll each mushroom cap in the butter, making sure all sides are covered. Leave them in the pan, cap sides down. Melt the remaining 3 tablespoons butter in a medium-sized skillet and sauté the garlic and minced mushroom stems for 5 minutes. Stir in the green pepper and pimiento and sauté another 3 minutes. Remove from heat and stir in the remaining ingredients. Heap the mixture into the mushroom caps. Bake 20 minutes. *Makes 12.*

Can be frozen. Freeze unbaked on a foil baking tray; thaw overnight in refrigerator. Grease jelly-roll pan and bake as above, omitting sherry.

CLAM-STUFFED MUSHROOMS

2 teaspoons sesame seeds
12 mushrooms, about 2 inches in diameter
2 tablespoons butter
1 clove garlic, crushed
3 ounces cream cheese
1 7½-ounce can minced clams, drained
¾ teaspoon Worcestershire sauce
¾ teaspoon grated onion
¼ teaspoon salt
¼ teaspoon freshly ground black pepper
1½ teaspoons chopped chives
¼ teaspoon dried oregano
½ egg yolk, beaten
½ teaspoon baking powder
2 tablespoons melted butter

Toast the sesame seeds in a 300° oven for 10 minutes. Raise oven heat to 375°. Wipe the mushrooms with a damp towel and gently ease the stems off, reserving stems for other use. In a large heavy skillet, melt the 2 tablespoons butter, add the garlic, and cook for 2 minutes. Remove the pan from the heat. Dip each mushroom cap in the garlic butter, making sure that the entire cap is coated. Grease a jelly-roll pan or baking dish with 2 tablespoons melted butter, put in the mushrooms, cap side down, and reserve. Let the cheese soften to room temperature. Add the clams, Worcestershire sauce, grated onion, salt, pepper, chives, and oregano. Combine thoroughly. Add the beaten yolk and the baking powder. Pile the mixture into the mushroom caps and sprinkle with toasted sesame seeds. Place the filled caps on the dish and bake 20 minutes. *Makes 12.*

Can be frozen. Follow directions for Christmas Mushrooms.

CRAB-STUFFED MUSHROOMS

12 large mushrooms, about 2 inches in diameter
9 tablespoons butter
1 clove garlic, crushed
2 tablespoonse finely minced shallots
1 tablespoon dry sherry
½ teaspoon salt
⅛ teaspoon freshly ground black pepper
1 tablespoon minced parsley
1 tablespoon chopped chives
1 teaspoon dried tarragon
1 cup crabmeat
1 egg, beaten
4 tablespoons bread crumbs
2 tablespoons freshly grated Parmesan cheese

Preheat oven to 350°. Wipe the mushrooms with a damp towel and gently ease the stems off. Reserve stems. In a large heavy skillet, melt 5 tablespoons of the butter, add the garlic, and cook for 2 minutes. Remove the pan from the heat. Dip each mushroom cap in the garlic butter, making sure that the entire cap is coated. Reserve garlic butter in skillet. Grease a jelly-roll pan or baking dish with 2 tablespoons butter, put in the mushrooms, cap side down, and reserve. Chop the mushroom stems fine. Reheat the garlic butter and sauté the mushroom stems and the shallots for 10 minutes. Add the sherry, raise the heat, and cook 2 minutes. Put the stem mixture into a large mixing bowl. Add the salt, pepper, parsley, chives, tarragon, crabmeat, beaten egg, and 2 tablespoons of the bread crumbs. Combine well. Pile the mixture into the mushroom caps. Melt 2 tablespoons of the remaining butter and sauté the remaining bread crumbs until well coated. Add grated Parmesan cheese and mix. Place ½ teaspoon of this mixture on top of each mushroom cap. Bake for 20 minutes. *Makes 12.*

Can be frozen. Follow directions for Mushrooms Roma, omitting sherry.

Hot Seafood

Since the main course of a dinner is likely to be meat or poultry, a hot seafood hors d'oeuvre will complement the central effort. For a large cocktail party, a hot meat and a hot fish dish are good choices.

CLAM BALLS

> 2 8-ounce cans minced clams
> 1 tablespoon bacon fat
> 2 teaspoons minced shallots
> 2 cloves garlic, minced (1 teaspoon)
> 1 tablespoon plus 1½ teaspoons flour
> ½ cup heavy cream
> 1 teaspoon dried oregano
> 2 teaspoons parsley
> ½ teaspoon Worcestershire sauce
> 4 dashes Tabasco
> ¼ teaspoon salt
> oil for deep frying

Drain the clams, reserving the liquid. You will have about 1 cup liquid and 1 cup clam meat. Melt the bacon fat in a skillet and sauté the shallots and garlic for about 3 minutes. Off the heat, blend in the flour, stirring until it is all incorporated. Add ¼ cup of the clam liquid and the cream gradually, stirring constantly. Return to heat and cook over moderate heat until the sauce is very thick. Remove from heat and add the remaining ingredients. Fold in the clams. Refrigerate the mixture at least 4 hours. With a ½ teaspoon measure form balls about ½ inch in diameter. Place on waxed paper. In a small heavy skillet pour oil to a depth of 1 inch and heat to 365°. Drop in 3 balls at a time, frying about 1 minute. Remove with slotted spoon and drain on paper towels. These can be kept warm in a 200° oven. If made in advance, reheat in a 425° oven placed on a wire rack in a jelly-roll pan for 7 minutes. *Makes 20.*

Can be frozen. Place on flat surface to freeze, then put into a freezer bag and seal. Reheat frozen balls in a 350° oven for 10 minutes as above.

CLAM PUFFS

2 8-ounce cans minced clams
1 egg, separated
½ cup flour
1 teaspoon baking powder
¾ teaspoon salt
3 dashes Tabasco
1 tablespoon melted butter
2 tablespoons reserved clam liquid
1 tablespoon chopped chives
1 tablespoon chopped fresh dill
oil for deep frying

Drain the clams, reserving 2 tablespoons of the liquid. Combine the drained clams, reserved liquid, the egg yolk, and the remaining ingredients except the egg white and the oil. Beat the egg white until stiff and fold into the mixture. Cover and chill at least 1 hour or overnight. Heat the oil in a deep-fryer to 375°. Drop the mixture into the fat by generous half-teaspoonfuls. Fry 4 or 5 at a time for 4 to 5 minutes, turning once. Drain on paper towels. Keep warm in a 200° oven until all are cooked.

These can be served on a platter around a small bowl of Remoulade Sauce (see index). *Makes about 24.*

Can be frozen. Thaw 1 hour. To reheat, place on a rack placed on a jelly-roll pan. Heat in a preheated 425° oven for 5 minutes.

BLUE-CLAM ROUNDS

¼ pound blue cheese
½ teaspoon Worcestershire sauce
1 tablespoon lemon juice
1 8-ounce can minced clams, drained
1 tablespoon grated onion
1 clove garlic, crushed
⅛ teaspoon freshly ground pepper
12 1½-inch Melba Toast rounds (see index)

Preheat oven to 350°. Let the cheese come to room temperature. Add all the other ingredients except the toast, and mix well. Spread ½ teaspoon of the mixture on each toast round. Place the rounds on a baking sheet and heat 10 minutes. Broil for 1 minute. *Makes 12.*

Can be frozen. Reheat, frozen, in a 375° oven for 15 minutes, then broil for 1 minute.

STUFFED CLAMS AMALFI

After tasting countless versions of stuffed clams I found that the seasoning always overpowered the delicate flavor of the clam itself. When I enjoyed these morsels at home, I enhanced them with nothing more than a squirt of lemon juice and a few grinds of pepper. Lunching on a glorious spring day in the Hotel Cappucchino (a converted monastery on the Amalfi Drive overlooking the Mediterranean), I tasted the clam that was part of my hot antipasto. After one bite I was ready to eat a whole meal of these subtly herbed creations.

60 cherrystone clams
¼ cup olive oil
¼ cup finely chopped shallots
4 cloves garlic, minced (2 teaspoons)
¼ cup fine dry bread crumbs
2 tablespoons finely chopped parsley
½ teaspoon dried oregano
½ teaspoon dried basil
1 teaspoon salt
½ teaspoon freshly ground black pepper
2 tablespoons reserved clam juice
2 tablespoons dry white wine

TOPPING
¼ cup fine dry bread crumbs
1 tablespoon freshly grated Parmesan cheese
4 tablespoons olive oil

Preheat oven to 375°. Have the clams shucked or open them yourself. Reserve the juices and 24 of the shells. Coarsely chop the meat with a large knife (do not use a blender or food processor) and put it into a mixing bowl. (There should be 1⅓ cups chopped clams.) Heat the ¼ cup oil in a small heavy skillet. Sauté the shallots and garlic over moderate heat for about 3 minutes or until they have softened. Pour them into the bowl with the clams. Add ¼ cup bread crumbs, the parsley, oregano, basil, salt, pepper, wine and 2 tablespoons reserved clam juice. Put about 1 tablespoon of the filling in each clam shell. Combine ¼ cup bread crumbs and the Parmesan cheese and sprinkle over each filled shell. Dribble ½ teaspoon oil over each. Place the filled shells on a jellyroll pan. Bake in a preheated 375° oven for 20 minutes. Run under the broiler for a minute if you want a browner crust. Serve with small forks. *Makes 24.*

Note: For a thrifty version, instead of fresh clams, use two 8-ounce cans of minced clams. Drain them and reserve the juice. Proceed as with the fresh clams.

Can be frozen. Freeze before baking, on foil pans. When frozen, place in plastic freezer bags and seal securely. To heat, place frozen in preheated 400° oven and bake for 20 minutes. Run under the broiler if desired.

GREEK-STYLE CRAB BALLS
(Mary's Crab Keftaides)

Although *keftaides* usually means meatballs, my friend Mary, who is of Greek ancestry on both sides, makes a version of a crab ball that she also calls *keftaides*. Like their meat namesake, these have an airy texture and delicate flavor, and they always disappear like clouds of smoke.

> 1 pound fresh crabmeat (not frozen)
> 2 hard-cooked eggs, chopped
> 2 tablespoons finely minced scallion
> 2 tablespoons finely chopped parsley
> 2 tablespoons Worcestershire sauce
> 2 teaspoons grated lemon rind
> ⅛ teaspoon white pepper
> ½ teaspoon salt
> 1 egg, beaten
> 2 tablespoons heavy cream
> flour
> oil for deep frying

Pick over and flake the crabmeat. Add all the other ingredients. Chill, covered, for a few hours. Roll the mixture into balls about the size of a quarter, using a measuring tablespoon. Roll each ball in flour. Preheat oven to 250°. Line a baking sheet with paper towels. Heat oil in a deep fryer to 375°. Fry the balls, four at a time, until golden. Place the balls in the oven on the paper towels until all are fried. These can be made a day in advance and reheated. Preheat oven to 425°. Place a wire rack on a jelly-roll pan, and place the balls on the rack. Bake for 10 minutes. *Makes 24.*

Can be frozen. Freeze on a flat surface. When frozen, put into a plastic bag and seal. To reheat, place on the rack over jelly-roll pan and heat at 425° for 20 minutes.

TAHITI CRAB BALLS

1 6½-ounce can crabmeat
1 tablespoon butter
1 tablespoon flour
½ cup milk
1 clove garlic, put through press (½ teaspoon)
1 teaspoon onion juice
½ teaspoon salt
3 dashes Tabasco
1 teaspoon curry powder
1 egg
2 tablespoons flour
1 4-ounce can shredded coconut
peanut oil

Drain the crabmeat. Melt the butter in a small, heavy saucepan. Off the heat, blend in the 1 tablespoon flour and slowly add the milk, whisking constantly. Add the garlic, onion juice, salt, Tabasco, and curry powder. Stir over moderate heat until the sauce thickens. Remove from heat and stir in the crabmeat. Put the mixture into a bowl, cover with plastic wrap, and refrigerate at least 3 hours or overnight.

Using a measuring teaspoon, form balls about 1 inch in diameter; place them on waxed paper. In a small bowl, lightly beat the egg. Stir in the 2 tablespoons flour until the batter is well blended. Spread the coconut on a sheet of waxed paper. Dip the crab balls into the batter, roll in coconut, and place on wire racks. Let dry 15 minutes.

Pour peanut oil into a small saucepan to a depth of 1 inch. Heat until the temperature of the fat reaches 365°, then drop 3 balls at a time into the fat. Turn them after 1 minute. Fry each ball 2 minutes in all. Remove with slotted spoon and drain on paper towels. These can be kept warm in a 200° oven. Serve with toothpicks. If made in advance, reheat for 7 minutes in a 425° oven on a wire rack in a jelly-roll pan. *Makes 15.*

Can be frozen. Place on flat surface to freeze. When frozen, put into a freezer bag and seal. Reheat frozen balls as above in a 350° oven for 20 minutes.

CAROLINA LOW COUNTRY CRAB BROIL

These tiny open-faced sandwiches are easy to serve and can be handled even while holding a drink. They can be made in advance; because they are heated before serving they do not become soggy.

    4 slices thin-sliced oatmeal bread
    1 6½-ounce can crabmeat
    ¼ cup mayonnaise
    3 tablespoons finely chopped celery
    2 tablespoons finely chopped black olives
    1 tablespoon lemon juice
    ¼ teaspoon salt
    1 clove garlic, put through press
    2 slices Swiss cheese

Preheat oven to 350°. Trim the crusts from the bread and cut each slice into quarters. Place on baking sheet and bake 10 minutes, turn, and bake an additional 5 minutes. Rinse the crabmeat in cold water and drain thoroughly. Combine with the mayonnaise, celery, olives, lemon juice, salt, and garlic. Cover each square of toast with some of the crab mixture. Cut the Swiss cheese into squares the size of the toast and place one on top of each sandwich. Place the squares on a baking sheet and bake for 15 minutes. Place under the broiler for a minute to brown. These may be made 2 or 3 hours in advance and refrigerated, before baking. *Makes 16.*

    Can be frozen. Freeze on a flat surface. Bake frozen in a preheated 350° oven for 25 minutes and then broil for a minute.

LOBSTER TOASTS

¼ pound lobster meat (¾ cup)
1 3-ounce package cream cheese with chives
2 tablespoons chopped chives
½ teaspoon salt
¼ teaspoon white pepper
¼ teaspoon Fines Herbes (Spice Islands)
1 tablespoon lemon juice
12 1½-inch Melba Rounds (see index)
2 tablespoons grated Parmesan cheese

Preheat oven to 375°. Shred the lobster meat. Let the cream cheese soften to room temperature. Add the lobster meat, chives, salt, pepper, herbs, and lemon juice. Combine well. Cover each toast round with the mixture and sprinkle with the Parmesan cheese. *Makes 12.*

Bake the rounds 12 minutes. Broil 1 minute.

SMOKED OYSTER PUFFS

2 3⅔-ounce cans smoked oysters
½ cup clam broth
¾ cup flour
2 eggs
2 teaspoons Worcestershire sauce
2 teaspoons onion juice
2 cloves garlic, put through press (1 teaspoon)
½ teaspoon salt
¼ teaspoon freshly ground pepper
2 tablespoons chopped chives
½ teaspoon lemon rind

Drain the oysters, reserving the oil. Chop the oysters coarsely. Lightly butter 2 baking sheets. Preheat oven to 450°. Place ¼ cup oil from oysters and ½ cup clam broth in a saucepan. Bring to a boil over low heat. Remove from heat, add the flour, and stir vigorously. Return the pan to low heat and beat until the mixture leaves the sides of the pan and forms a ball. Cool for a few minutes. Place the mixture in the bowl of an electric mixer. Add the eggs, one at a time, beating well after each addition. Fold in the smoked oysters, and all the remaining ingredients. Using a measuring teaspoon, drop mounds of the mixture on the baking sheets. Bake at 450° for 10 minutes, then reduce heat to 350° and bake an additional 5 minutes. If made in advance, reheat at 350° for 5 to 8 minutes. *Makes about 40.*

Can be frozen. Freeze the baked puffs on a flat surface, then pack in foil pans and cover with a plastic bag. Place frozen puffs on baking sheets and reheat at 350° for 10 to 15 minutes.

PUFFY SCALLOP BITES

> 1 pound sea scallops, poached in water for 5 minutes
> 2 tablespoons Duxelles (see index)
> ¼ cup mayonnaise
> 1 teaspoon lemon juice
> 1 tablespoon chopped chives
> 1 tablespoon chopped parsley
> 3 dashes cayenne pepper
> ⅛ teaspoon salt
> 1 egg white, stiffly beaten
> About 30 Melba Rounds (see index)

Preheat broiler. Drain the poached scallops and dry on paper towels. Cut in half horizontally. Place each on a Melba Round and place on baking sheet.

Combine the Duxelles, mayonnaise, lemon juice, chives, parsley, cayenne pepper, and salt. Fold in the beaten egg white. Place a spoonful of the mixture on top of each scallop and broil until puffy and golden. Watch carefully, as these burn quickly. Serve immediately. *Makes about 30.*

SCAMPI-STYLE SHRIMP

Unless you are dining in Venice or its environs, chances are that the *scampi* on the menu will really be jumbo shrimp. True scampi are native to the Adriatic and are more closely related to the French *langoustine* and the Dublin Bay prawn than any of these are to

American shrimp. However, the basic ingredients used by the Venetians in preparing this delicacy, when applied to American shrimp, produce an aromatic dish. To be truly authentic, one should marinate the shrimp in their shells and then broil them. For cocktail service, however, this shelled version is safer.

1 pound jumbo shrimp, about 20

MARINADE
1 cup olive oil
1 tablespoon finely chopped parsley
1 teaspoon salt
18 cloves garlic, finely chopped (about 3 tablespoons)
4 shallots finely chopped (2 tablespoons)
¼ cup Chablis
⅛ teaspoon dried crushed red pepper
2 tablespoons chopped chives

Shell and devein the shrimp. Wash them and dry on paper towels. Combine all the marinade ingredients except the chives. Put the shrimp in an ovenproof baking dish just large enough to hold them. Pour the marinade over them and turn them to coat them on all sides. Cover with plastic wrap and refrigerate for 8 hours or overnight. Remove from the refrigerator about half an hour before you plan to serve them. Preheat oven to 450°. Just before your guests arrive, place the dish in the oven and bake for 12 minutes, turning and basting the shrimp after 6 minutes. Transfer them to a chafing dish and sprinkle with the chives. Provide toothpicks and have a basket of small slices of Italian or French bread nearby so guests can spear the shrimp and also enjoy the garlicky sauce. Unless you are having a very large gathering, do not cook more than one batch at a time; they tend to toughen in the chafing dish. You can adjust the amount of garlic up or down—my family prefers even a bit more. *Makes about 20.*

SHRIMP IN BEER BATTER

As soon as the Four Seasons restaurant opened in New York it drew enthusiastic comment on its innovative cuisine. The genius largely responsible was the late Albert Stockli. One much-discussed dish was fried shrimp stuffed with a cream sauce laced with Italian mustard fruit. In this dish Stockli did not use the beer batter that he popularized for many other dishes, but when serving it as a finger food, I prefer to use my version of Beer Batter and a dip of puréed *mostarda di frutta*, a specialty produced in Cremona, Italy, and available in gourmet or Italian food stores.

Beer Batter (see following recipe)
24 large shrimp, peeled, with tail shell left on
½ cup lemon juice
2 teaspoons curry powder
flour
oil for deep-frying

Make the batter several hours in advance, or the previous day. Marinate the shrimp in the lemon juice and curry powder for 30 minutes. Heat the oil in a deep-fryer to 375°. Just before using the batter, add 1 tablespoon hot oil from fryer and whisk batter again. Drain and dry the shrimp. Coat each shrimp in flour, shaking off the excess, and dip in the batter, holding by the unshelled tail. Fry 6 at a time for 3 to 4 minutes or until golden. Turn them as they fry. Remove them with a slotted spoon and drain on paper towels. Keep them warm in a 250° oven on cookie sheets covered with paper towels while frying the rest. Serve on a lettuce-lined platter with a bowl of Italian Mustard Fruit Sauce (see index) in the center. The tails serve as handles.

Shrimp or other shellfish in beer batter can be fried in advance and reheated. Preheat oven to 425°. Place a wire rack on a jelly-roll pan and put the seafood on the rack and bake about 5 to 7 minutes. *Makes 24.*

Can be frozen. Freeze on a flat surface, then put into a plastic bag and seal. To reheat, preheat oven to 425°. Put the frozen shellfish on a rack as described above. Bake shrimp, oysters, or mussels 15 minutes; crab claws, 20 minutes.

OTHER SHELLFISH IN BEER BATTER

Medium-sized crab claws, each one about two bites, are becoming easier to find fresh in fish markets or frozen at the supermarket. Defrost if frozen. Dry the claws thoroughly and dip them into the flour and then the beer batter, holding them by the unshelled ends. Fry as in main recipe for about 4 to 5 minutes and keep warm. Serve with Chinese Fish Sauce (see index) as a dip.

Oysters or steamed mussels can also be fried in Beer Batter. Marinate them for 30 minutes in ½ cup lemon juice and a few drops of Tabasco. Dry thoroughly, dip in flour, and then, holding with tongs, dip each in the batter. Fry 3 or 4 minutes.

All these can be frozen; see main recipe.

SAUSAGE AND CHEESE IN BEER BATTER

Once when I needed a quick cocktail accompaniment for unexpected guests I was lucky enough to have a bowl of leftover beer batter in the refrigerator. I cut cubes of salami and Gruyère cheese, rolled braunschweiger into balls, and dipped all in the batter. I fried them for about 5 minutes, then served them with a bowl of Mustard Mayonnaise (see index) diluted with a bit of sour cream.

BEER BATTER

This amount of batter is more than enough to coat 24 shrimp or a dozen crab claws, or oysters, or mussels. It also works well for meat or vegetables. The batter will keep for a week in the refrigerator and can be reused as long as it lasts, but once a batch has been used for fish, keep it only for fish.

> 1 cup sifted flour
> ½ teaspoon baking powder
> 2 teaspoons salt
> pinch cayenne pepper
> 1 cup flat beer
> 1 tablespoon vegetable oil

Put the sifted flour in a bowl. Add the baking powder, salt, and cayenne pepper. Slowly add the beer, whisking until you have a smooth batter. Whisk in the oil and mix until it is all incorporated. Cover the bowl and let the batter rest at least 2 hours at room temperature or refrigerate overnight. Before using, vigorously whisk again.

ITALIAN MUSTARD FRUIT SAUCE

    1 cup *mostarda di frutta di Cremona*
    ¼ cup orange juice
    ¼ cup lemon juice

In an electric blender or food processor, purée the mustard fruit. You will have ½ cup purée. Add the orange and lemon juices and blend again. Make three days in advance and refrigerate. Bring to room temperature before serving. *Makes 1 cup.*

CHINESE FISH SAUCE

    5 tablespoons sour cream
    1 tablespoon Chinese oyster sauce
    few dashes cayenne pepper

Mix all ingredients. May be made 24 hours in advance and refrigerated.

CHINESE SHRIMP TOAST

For years I minced the shrimp for this with a cleaver; with a food processor the paste is ready in a matter of minutes to be used either on toast or as balls.

10 slices 2-day-old thin-sliced white bread
1 pound raw shrimp (¾ pound shelled)
1 small onion
2 cloves garlic
6 water chestnuts
1½ teaspoons grated fresh ginger
2 teaspoons dry sherry
1 teaspoon salt
¼ teaspoon freshly ground black pepper
1 teaspoon sugar
¼ teaspoon sesame oil
4 tablespoons cornstarch
2 tablespoons soy sauce
2 eggs, lightly beaten
2 cups peanut oil

Trim crusts off bread. Cut each slice into 4 triangles. (If bread is fresh, trim off the crusts, cut it into triangles, and bake it in a 300° oven for 10 minutes. Very fresh bread will soak up too much oil and not become crisp.) Shell and devein shrimp. Wash and drain. With a food processor, coarsely chop the shrimp and onion, and add to the bowl the whole garlic cloves, the water chestnuts, and the ginger. Run for a minute. Add all the rest of the ingredients except the peanut oil, and process just until you have a smooth mixture. If you do not have a food processor, mince the shrimp in a wooden bowl. Finely chop onion and water chestnuts. Transfer shrimp, onion, and water chestnuts to a large glass bowl. Mince the garlic very fine. Add sherry, salt, pepper, sugar, ginger, garlic, sesame oil, cornstarch, and soy sauce. Mix well. Add the lightly beaten eggs. Blend thoroughly. Spread mixture on the triangles of bread, heaping high to the edges. Heat peanut oil in a large skillet or deep-fryer to 375°. Place the bread in the oil, shrimp side down, about 10 at a time. Fry until edges are golden brown. Turn and brown the bottom of the bread for about 30 seconds. Remove with a slotted spoon and drain on paper towels. Serve hot. The triangles can be kept warm for a few minutes in a pre-heated 200° oven on paper towel lined pan. *Makes 40 pieces.*

Can be frozen. Reheat in a 425° oven on a wire rack placed in a jelly-roll pan—about 10 minutes if frozen, about 5 minutes if thawed.

COCKTAIL FISH FINGERS

Many sauces go well with these; among my favorites are Green Goddess Dressing, Remoulade Sauce, Homemade Duck Sauce, Velvety Cocktail Sauce, and Tartare Sauce (see index).

> 1 pound fish fillets, preferably firm
>   white fish such as cod or haddock
> juice of 1 lemon
> oil for deep frying
> ½ cup flour
> ½ teaspoon salt
> ½ recipe Beer Batter (see index)
> 2 tablespoons hot oil from fryer

Cut the fillets into strips about 2 inches long and 1½ inches wide and thick. Put them in a glass or ceramic bowl and sprinkle them with lemon juice. Cover the bowl securely with plastic wrap and refrigerate for about 1 hour. Heat the oil in a deep-fryer to 375°. In a plastic bag, combine the flour and salt. Put the fish pieces in the bag and shake to coat them. Add 2 tablespoons hot oil to batter. Holding the strips with tongs, dip them one by one in the batter. In the hot oil fry a few pieces at a time for about 4 minutes, turning them to ensure even browning. Drain them on paper towels. As you finish each batch, put them in a 200° oven on paper towel lined pan until all are fried. The same method can be used to cook larger pieces of fish for a main course.

These can be made ahead and reheated. Preheat oven to 425.° Put fish on a jelly-roll pan and bake 5 minutes. *Makes about 36.*

Can be frozen. Freeze on flat surface or directly on foil pans, then cover with a plastic bag and seal. To reheat, place fingers on rack and heat as described above for 12 minutes.

SWEDISH FISH TOAST

If the Chinese can have shrimp toast, why not a more economical fish toast? I call this Swedish because mixtures of white fish and dill are so much a part of Swedish cuisine.

12 slices 2-day-old thin-sliced white bread
1 pound cod fillets or other white-fleshed fish
¼ cup lemon juice
5 tablespoons minced shallots
5 tablespoons coarsely chopped fresh dill
2 teaspoons salt
¼ teaspoon Tabasco
2 tablespoons cornstarch
2 tablespoons dry sherry
2 egg whites
2 cups vegetable oil for deep frying

Trim the crusts off each slice of bread and cut into four triangles. (If very fresh bread is used, trim off the crusts, cut each slice into triangles and bake in a 300° oven for 10 minutes. Fresh bread will soak up too much oil and not become crisp.) Soak the fish in the lemon juice in a covered glass bowl in the refrigerator for 1 hour. Drain and dry. If you have a food processor, use it to mince the shallots. Cut the fish into 1-inch cubes and add. Put in the dill, coarsely chopped, the salt, and Tabasco. Process for a few seconds. Add the cornstarch, sherry, and egg whites and run the machine only to combine. You want a coarsely textured paste, not a real pureé. If you do not have a food processor, mince the fish fine in a wooden bowl. Add the minced shallots, finely chopped dill, salt, Tabasco, cornstarch, sherry, and egg whites, and stir to combine. Spread the mixture on the bread triangles, heaping high and covering the entire surface. Heat the oil in a large skillet or deep-fryer to 375°. Place the bread triangles in the oil, fish side down. Fry a few at a time until the edges of the bread are golden brown. Turn and brown the bottom of the bread for about 30 seconds. Remove with a slotted spoon and drain on paper towels. Serve hot. These can be kept warm in a preheated 200° oven on paper towels for a few minutes. *Makes 48.*

Can be frozen. See Chinese Shrimp Toast.

FISH BALLS
Instead of using bread, drop mixture by tablespoons into the hot fat and fry for about 3 minutes. Serve with Green Goddess Dressing (see index). *Makes about 32 balls.*

SARDINE FINGERS

Because this recipe contains baking powder, it should be assembled at the last minute, but you can have the toast prepared and all the other ingredients ready.

    5 slices firm white bread
    4 tablespoons melted butter
    3 ounces cream cheese
    1 egg yolk
    ½ teaspoon baking powder
    ¼ teaspoon freshly ground black pepper
    2 tablespoons minced onion
    1 teaspoon Worcestershire sauce
    1 teaspoon grated lemon rind
    1 3¾-ounce can Swedish Brisling sardines
    paprika

Preheat oven to 350°. Cut crusts off bread; cut into 1-inch-wide strips. Brush both sides with melted butter. Place on a baking sheet. Bake 7 minutes.

Increase oven heat to 375°. Let the cream cheese soften to room temperature in the mixing bowl of an electric mixer or the bowl of a food processor. Beat the cheese, beat in the egg yolk, baking powder, pepper, onion, Worcestershire sauce, and lemon rind. Drain the sardines on paper towels. Place a sardine on each toast finger. Cover with the cheese mixture up to the edges. Sprinkle with paprika. Bake 12 minutes and then run under broiler for 1 minute. *Makes 15.*

ANCHOVY FINGERS

Makes toast strips as for Sardine Fingers. Follow previous instructions, except use only 1 tablespoon minced onion, omit Worcestershire sauce and lemon, and add a dash of Tabasco. Substitute a 2-ounce can of anchovy fillets for the sardines, cut each anchovy in half, and place 3 halves on each strip. Spread with the cheese mixture and sprinkle with 3 tablespoons grated Cheddar cheese.

SARDINE TOASTS

4 small white onions
1 3-ounce package cream cheese with chives
1 egg yolk
½ teaspoon baking powder
2 dashes Worcestershire sauce
2 grinds black pepper
12 1½-inch Melba Rounds (see index)
1 3¾-ounce can skinless and boneless sardines,
　　drained and mashed

Preheat oven to 375°. Peel the onions and cut into ¼-inch slices. Let the cream cheese soften in the mixing bowl of an electric mixer. Beat the cheese, beat in the egg yolk, baking powder, Worcestershire sauce, and pepper. Cover each round with ¼ teaspoon mashed sardines. Top each with a slice of onion and then 1 teaspoon of the cheese mixture.

Bake 12 minutes, then broil 1 minute. *Makes 12.*

SHRIMP TOASTS

Omit onion slices, and add 1 teaspoon onion juice to the cheese mixture. Cut 12 medium-sized, cooked shrimp in half, place 2 halves on each toast round, and cover with the cheese mixture.

Hot
Meats and Poultry

Most Americans are meat eaters, despite the recent increase in the number of vegetarians and other meat abstainers. Hot meat hors d'oeuvres need not be limited to meatballs or cocktail frankfurters, welcome though these are; a wide variety of choices is available and most do not require expensive cuts. Almost all may be made in advance and reheated, and many freeze successfully. However, except for a large party, one meat hors d'oeuvre is enough.

MIXED BAG

This assortment of recipes offers guests an interesting variety of crisp morsels to dip in a pungent sauce. They will probably make repeated forays to the hors d'oeuvres table to try the different taste sensations provided. This treatment can be used not only for pork cubes, chicken livers, and shrimp but also for scallops, sausages, and even water chestnuts. The sauce was inspired by Rose Gray, a delightful Chinese lady who teaches cooking in the Adult Education Department of the Westport, Connecticut, school system. Most of her dishes are authentically Chinese, learned from her mother and grandmother in China, but this sauce shows some American influences. You can put all the tidbits in the sauce and let them wait in a chafing dish, but I prefer to serve the bites and sauce separately to retain the crunch of the coating. I put the bites on a warming tray and keep the sauce hot in a small chafing dish or in a bowl over a candle warmer. Have plenty of toothpicks handy.

Pork Cubes

> 1 pound lean, boneless pork, cut in 1-inch cubes
> 2 teaspoons salt
> ¼ teaspoon freshly ground black pepper
> ¼ cup cornstarch
> ½ cup peanut oil
> ½ cup sesame oil

Put the pork cubes on waxed paper and sprinkle all over with the salt and pepper. Let stand 1 hour. Preheat oven to 200°. Put the cornstarch in a plastic bag and shake the cubes in it to coat. Shake off any excess. In a large heavy skillet, heat the oils until almost smoking. Drop in the cubes and turn them quickly to give them a nice crust. Lower the heat to medium and sauté the cubes until they are no longer pink inside—usually about 5 minutes. Remove with a slotted spoon and drain on paper towels. Keep cubes warm on paper towel lined baking sheet in the oven while you are cooking the other tidbits. *Makes about 20.*

Chicken Livers

> 1 pound chicken livers, washed, drained, dried,
>   and cut in half

Put the chicken liver pieces on waxed paper and sprinkle all over with salt and pepper. Let stand for ½ hour. Prepare as pork cubes but sauté over medium heat only 4 minutes, leaving centers still juicy and slightly pink. *Makes about 32.*

Shrimp

> 1 pound raw shrimp, shelled and deveined

Wash the shrimp and dry them on paper towels. Sprinkle them all over with 1 teaspoon salt and ¼ teaspoon white pepper. Let stand 1 hour.

Preheat oven to 425°. Follow previous instructions, but sauté quickly over high heat until just pink and still juicy—about 3 minutes. *Makes about 20.*

Note: All these can be made in advance and reheated. Place a rack on a jelly-roll pan. Put bites on rack and bake in a 200° oven for 5 minutes.

Can be frozen. Freeze on a flat surface, then place in a plastic freezer bag and seal tightly. To reheat, thaw overnight in the refrigerator. Put on a rack placed on a jelly-roll pan. Bake in a preheated 425° oven for 10 minutes.

Rosie's Sauce

Prepare the sauce while the tidbits are marinating. It can also be made a day before and reheated, but do not add the scallions until serving time.

¾ cup orange juice
4 teaspoons curry powder
1 cup tomato sauce
½ cup light soy sauce
½ cup sugar
10 cloves garlic, finely minced (3 tablespoons)
4 teaspoons sesame oil
¼ cup rice wine (*shao-hsing*) or dry sherry
½ cup chopped scallions

In a saucepan, combine all the ingredients except the scallions and heat just to dissolve and blend the seasonings. Sprinkle with scallions just before serving. *Makes about 3 cups.*

MIDAS STEAK SQUARES

These are among the easiest tidbits to prepare, especially on an outdoor barbecue. Their one drawback is the cost of the main ingredient, but when you want to splurge they are sure to please.

2 1½-inch-thick pieces tenderloin or
  sirloin strip (about 1 pound)
1 cup olive oil
4 cloves garlic, crushed (1 teaspoon)

SAUCE
½ pound butter
12 shallots chopped (about 6 tablespoons)
8 cloves garlic, finely minced (4 tablespoons)
4 teaspoons Worcestershire sauce
1½ teaspoons Dijon mustard
4 tablespoons Burgundy
1 tablespoon chopped fresh parsley
1 tablespoon chopped fresh chives

Marinate the steak in the olive oil and 4 cloves crushed garlic for
2 hours at room temperature, turning it every half hour. Prepare
the sauce by melting the butter in a medium-sized saucepan. Add
the shallots and 8 cloves minced garlic and sauté for 3 minutes.
Add the Worcestershire sauce, mustard, and wine. Simmer for 5
minutes. Keep hot in a chafing dish while cooking the meat. Stir
in the parsley and chives just before serving. Broil the beef over
the fire or in the oven just until the outside is charred; the inside
should be very rare. Cut into 1-inch squares and rush to the wait-
ing sauce. Provide forks and small slices of French bread to ab-
sorb the juices and sauce. Do not cook the meat in advance; it
will get too well done in the sauce. *Makes about 22.*

ROSIE GRAY'S SCALLION BEEF ROLLS

½ pound flank steak or top round
1 egg white
1 teaspoon salt
1 teaspoon cornstarch
1 tablespoon fermented black beans, rinsed, dried,
  and minced
6 cloves garlic, minced (1 tablespoon)

1 tablespoon minced fresh ginger
½ teaspoon sugar
½ teaspoon monosodium glutamate (optional)
1 tablespoon light soy sauce
1 tablespoon red wine
8 scallions
1 teaspoon sesame oil

Slice the steak ¼ inch thick and 2 inches square. Pound it lightly until it is about ⅛-inch thick. Combine the egg white, salt, and cornstarch, and marinate the meat in this mixture while preparing the rest of the ingredients. Mix together the black beans, garlic, ginger, sugar, monosodium glutamate (if used), soy sauce, and red wine. Blend this mixture well and set aside. Wash the scallions, trim off the bases, and cut the white part into 2-inch lengths. Put the green parts of the scallions in a bowl and pour boiling water over them. Drain immediately and dry on paper towels. Lay the beef squares flat and spread ¾ teaspoon of the bean mixture on each piece. Put one piece of white scallion on top and roll up the beef tightly. Secure each bundle with one or two strips of the green parts of the scallions, tying it on top. Brush the rolls with the sesame oil. Broil them 1 minute on each side. Serve immediately. *Makes 8.*

CARIBBEAN FIREBALLS

4 tablespoons brown sugar
2 teaspoons dark mustard
2 teaspoons flour
2 8-ounce cans cocktail meatballs
1 cup light rum
½ teaspoon allspice
½ teaspoon nutmeg
1 teaspoon cinnamon
½ cup chicken stock (if needed)
2 tablespoons minced parsley

Mix the brown sugar, mustard, and flour into a thick paste. Put the meatballs, with their gravy, into a 10- to 12-inch skillet. Add the brown-sugar paste and ½ cup of the rum. Stir over medium heat until this has dissolved into gravy. Add the allspice, nutmeg, and cinnamon. Keep at a brisk simmer until mixture bubbles (about 10 minutes). (The recipe can be made in advance up to this point. In that case, reheat for a few minutes before proceeding.) Add the remaining rum and cook for 2 minutes more. If the sauce is too thick, add chicken stock. Before serving, sprinkle with the parsley. *Makes about 12–16 depending on brand and size of meatballs.*

Note: The meatballs can be heated in a chafing dish. In that case, add all the rum along with the brown-sugar paste. The process will take about 20 minutes in all. Alternatively, after the meatballs have been heated on the stove, they may be placed in a warmed chafing dish to keep hot. Stir occasionally so that neither meatballs nor sauce dry out.

FLIP'S CHINESE GARLIC MEATBALLS

Almost every nation has its own variety of meatballs; each nuance added by another culture makes it something special. Warning: Don't serve meatballs preceding a dinner in which the meat course contains similar ingredients.

    1½ pounds ground round beef
    ¾ cup soy sauce
    2 tablespoons dry sherry
    3 slices fresh ginger, minced (1 tablespoon)
    5 cloves garlic, finely minced (3 teaspoons)
    2 tablespoons sugar

Preheat oven to 350°. Combine all ingredients. Cover a jelly-roll pan with aluminum foil. Using a measuring teaspoon, make small balls of the mixture. Place the balls on the foil. Bake for 20 minutes. Place in a chafing dish, with cocktail picks and homemade Duck Sauce nearby for dipping. *Makes about 50.*

Can be frozen. Freeze on a flat surface, then place in a plastic freezer bag and seal securely. To serve, place frozen balls on a foil-lined baking sheet and bake in a 350° oven for 10 minutes.

GREEK MEATBALLS
(Keftaides)

These are usually served with the tangy egg-lemon sauce the Greeks call *avgolemeno*, but if the meatballs must wait in a chafing dish, the sauce tends to curdle, so I have created my own variation.

2 slices firm white bread, crusts removed
½ cup red wine
1 medium onion, minced (½ cup)
1 pound ground round beef
2 cloves garlic, put through a garlic press
2 tablespoons chopped fresh parsley
1 teaspoon dried oregano
2 teaspoons dried mint
1¼ teaspoon salt
¼ teaspoon freshly ground black pepper
1 teaspoon grated lemon peel
1 egg, beaten
¼ cup olive oil

SAUCE
2 tablespoons butter
3 tablespoons flour
⅔ cup light cream
1 10½-ounce can beef consommé
1½ cups grated Kasseri or Romano cheese
½ cup fresh chives, finely chopped

Crumble the bread and soak in the wine for 10 minutes. In a large mixing bowl combine the soaked bread and wine, the minced onion, beef, garlic, parsley, oregano, mint, salt, pepper, grated lemon peel, and egg. Blend mixture well with fingers. Cover bowl with plastic wrap and chill at least ½ hour. Wet palms with cold water. Using a measuring teaspoon form the mixture into small balls. In a heavy skillet heat the olive oil. Sauté the meatballs in two batches, shaking the pan to keep the balls round. As they are browned, remove with a slotted spoon to a heavy casserole.

For the sauce, melt the butter in a medium-sized heavy skillet. Off the heat blend in the flour, then return the skillet to the heat and stir constantly for 1 minute. Gradually add the cream and consommé, stirring constantly with a wire whisk. When all the liquid has blended with the flour, add the grated cheese and continue to stir until the cheese melts and the sauce thickens. Pour the sauce over the meatballs and simmer, covered, 10 minutes. Sprinkle with chives. *Makes 36.*

ITALIAN MEATBALLS
(Polpette)

½ pound ground chuck beef
½ pound ground veal
2 cloves garlic, finely minced (1 teaspoon)
1 teaspoon salt
¼ teaspoon freshly ground black pepper
½ teaspoon dried basil
½ teaspoon dried oregano
1 tablespoon finely minced parsley, preferably Italian
¼ teaspoon grated nutmeg
2 tablespoons grated Parmesan cheese
1 egg, beaten
2 tablespoons Italian seasoned bread crumbs

Combine all ingredients and chill 1 hour. Wet hands and roll into 1-inch balls. Preheat oven to 350°. Place balls on jelly-roll pan and bake 20 minutes, turning every 5 minutes. Serve in a chafing dish with the following sauce, or serve sauce as a dip. *Makes 24.*

Can be frozen. Freeze meatballs in sauce. Defrost overnight and reheat in a large saucepan.

Sauce for Italian Meatballs

2 tablespoons olive oil
¾ cup finely chopped onion
1 clove garlic, minced (½ teaspoon)
1 8-ounce can tomato sauce
¾ teaspoon Italian herb seasoning

Heat the olive oil in a saucepan and sauté the onion until golden.
Add the garlic and cook another 2 minutes. Add the tomato sauce
and Italian seasoning, bring to a boil, lower heat, and simmer 5
minutes.

SWEDISH MEATBALLS
(Kottbullar)

Nowadays Swedish meatballs are so popular that there are mixes
for them available, but since they are comparatively easy to prepare, why not do it yourself? Seasonings and sauces may vary, but
it is essential that the meat be very finely ground.

½ cup finely minced onion
2 cloves garlic, finely minced
3 tablespoons butter
¾ cup rye bread crumbs
¾ cup buttermilk
¾ pound round beef, ground twice
¼ pound veal, ground twice
¼ pound pork, ground twice
2 teaspoons salt
¼ teaspoon freshly ground black pepper
¼ teaspoon ground nutmeg
¼ teaspoon ground ginger
⅛ teaspoon allspice
1 tablespoon chopped fresh dill
2 eggs, lightly beaten
1 tablespoon bacon fat

Sauté onion and garlic in 1 tablespoon of the butter for about 5 minutes, just until soft. In a large bowl, soak the bread crumbs in the buttermilk for 5 minutes. Add the meats, the sautéed onion and garlic, salt, pepper, nutmeg, ginger, allspice, and dill. Add the beaten eggs. Combine mixture with hands. Cover bowl with plastic wrap and refrigerate for 1 hour. Wet palms with cold water. Form 1-inch balls, using a generous teaspoon of the mixture. As each is formed, place on a large jelly-roll pan covered with waxed paper. When all balls are formed, cover with additional waxed paper and refrigerate for another hour. In a heavy 12-inch skillet, melt the remaining 2 tablespoons butter and the bacon fat. When fat is quite hot, add about 12 of the meatballs. Shake the pan so the balls are quickly coated with fat and keep their round shape. After about 3 minutes, lower heat and brown them for another 5 minutes. Remove them with a slotted spoon to a heavy 3-quart casserole. Repeat with the rest of meatballs, about 12 at a time, adding more butter as necessary.

Make the gravy.

GRAVY
3 tablespoons butter
2 tablespoons flour
1 cup beef broth
3 tablespoons dry sherry
¾ cup light cream
½ teaspoon salt
⅛ teaspoon freshly ground black pepper
¼ teaspoon nutmeg
¼ teaspoon allspice
¼ teaspoon ginger
¼ teaspoon Maggi seasoning
¼ cup chopped fresh dill
1 tablespoon chopped fresh dill for garnish (optional)

In a medium-sized heavy casserole, melt the butter. Remove from heat, and blend in the flour. Gradually add the beef broth and sherry, stirring constantly with a wire whisk. When well blended, return to moderate heat and whisk constantly until the mixture thickens. Off the heat, blend in the remaining ingredients. Return to heat and simmer, stirring constantly, for 3 minutes.

Pour the gravy over the meatballs, cover, and simmer 5 minutes. If necessary to reheat, place in the top of a double boiler over simmering water or place in 325° oven for 20 minutes. Serve in a chafing dish or in a covered dish placed on a hot tray. Just before serving, sprinkle with the 1 tablespoon additional chopped dill if desired. *Makes 50.*

SWEDISH MEATBALLS IN BREAD CASE

3 tablespoons butter
¼ cup onion, finely chopped
¼ cup milk
2 slices white bread, crusts removed
1 pound round beef, ground twice
1 teaspoon salt
½ teaspoon freshly ground black pepper
1 teaspoon cloves
1 teaspoon ginger
1 teaspoon nutmeg
1 teaspoon allspice
1 egg, lightly beaten
1 teaspoon brown sugar
1 tablespoon bacon fat
1 10½-ounce can chicken broth
1 teaspoon Bovril
½ cup milk
2 teaspoons flour
1 small round loaf pumpernickel

In a small skillet, melt 1 tablespoon of the butter. Sauté onions until golden (about 10 minutes). Put into a large mixing bowl. Put the ¼ cup milk into a small bowl. Crumble the bread and soak it in the milk for 5 minutes. Add to onions. Add the beef, salt, pepper, cloves, ginger, nutmeg, allspice, egg, and brown sugar and mix to combine. Form small balls, using a measuring teaspoon and the palms of your hands, wet with cold water, to shape the balls. In a large heavy skillet, melt the remaining 2 tablespoons butter and the bacon fat. Brown the meatballs in two batches, shaking the pan to insure that they keep their shape. As they brown, remove them to paper towels.

In another large skillet, heat the chicken broth and Bovril, stirring until the Bovril dissolves. Bring to a boil and remove from heat. Stir in the ½ cup milk and the flour. Return skillet to heat and stir over low heat for a few minutes until sauce is smooth. Put in the meatballs and simmer, covered, for 1 hour, stirring occasionally. Cool balls in sauce and refrigerate or freeze for a few hours or up to 2 days.

Cut a slice off the top of the pumpernickel loaf; reserve this slice. Scoop out the center and put in the balls and sauce. Wrap bread in foil. Preheat oven to 350°. Put foil-wrapped bread on a baking sheet and bake 30 minutes. Remove foil and place loaf on a serving plate. Cover with reserved top slice. Serve with toothpicks or small forks. *Makes 28 balls.*

Can be frozen before placing in bread case. Freeze meat balls and sauce in a freezer container. Thaw overnight in refrigerator before placing in bread case.

KNOCKWURST IN BARBECUE SAUCE

4 knockwurst, about 1 pound
2 tablespoons butter
½ cup minced onions
4 cloves garlic, crushed (2 teaspoons)
2 tablespoons Worcestershire sauce
¼ cup red wine vinegar
¼ cup brown sugar
2 teaspoons Dijon mustard
2 teaspoons soy sauce
½ cup red pepper relish
1 cup Escoffier Sauce Diable
½ cup beer
½ cup catchup
2 dashes Tabasco sauce

In a saucepan, bring enough water to cover knockwurst to a boil. Add knockwurst and simmer 10 minutes. Remove. When knockwurst is cool enough to handle, peel, and cut into ¾-inch slices.

Melt the butter in a medium-sized saucepan. Add minced onion and garlic, and sauté about 5 minutes, stirring constantly. Off the heat, add the remaining ingredients and stir well to blend. Return to heat and cook at a low simmer, uncovered, for 20 minutes. Stir every 5 minutes. Add the knockwurst slices to the sauce and cook, covered, over low heat for 15 minutes, stirring every 5 minutes. Place over hot water in a chafing dish. Serve with toothpicks and napkins. *Makes about 36.*

Can be frozen. Place in freezer containers. Thaw overnight in refrigerator. Heat over simmering water in the top of a double boiler for 15 minutes.

CRUNCHY SAUSAGE BALLS

1 pound sausage meat
½ teaspoon salt
1 clove garlic, crushed (½ teaspoon)
½ teaspoon onion juice
¼ teaspoon freshly ground black pepper
½ teaspoon grated fresh ginger
1 tablespoon soy sauce
1 5-ounce can water chestnuts

Combine the sausage meat with the salt, garlic, onion juice, pepper, ginger, and soy sauce. Work in seasonings with fingers. Drain the water chestnuts. Cut each into quarters. Wrap a generous teaspoon of the sausage mixture around each piece of water chestnut, rolling between palms to make a smooth ball. Place balls on a jelly-roll pan or a shallow roasting pan with sides (fat from the sausage will melt). Each ball will be about 1 inch in diameter. Bake at 400° for 10 minutes, then carefully turn balls and bake another 10 minutes. Drain on paper towels. Serve with a toothpick inserted in each. Duck Sauce makes a good accompaniment. *Makes 30.*

Can be frozen. To reheat, place unthawed on cookie sheet and heat at 400° for about 10 minutes.

CHINESE PORK BALLS

The most famous Chinese meatball is the one called a pearl ball, for which the pork mixture is dipped in glutinous rice or sweet rice and then steamed. This recipe is a simplified version which retains the basic flavors of its elegant counterpart and uses ingredients that are easier to obtain.

½ pound ground pork
4 tablespoons finely chopped water chestnuts
4 tablespoons finely chopped scallions
1 clove garlic, finely chopped (½ teaspoon)
2 teaspoons grated fresh ginger
½ teaspoon salt
pinch freshly ground black pepper
½ teaspoon monosodium glutamate (optional)
pinch sugar
¼ cup soy sauce
2 teaspoons cornstarch dissolved in 2 teaspoons dry sherry
peanut oil

Combine all ingredients except the oil. Chill mixture. Line a large platter with waxed paper. Moisten palms with cold water. With a measuring teaspoon, pick up mixture and roll between wet palms into 1-inch balls. Place on the lined platter. Continue to make balls (24 in all), remoistening palms as necessary. Chill balls 1 hour. In a deep-fryer, pour peanut oil to a depth of 3 inches and heat to 350°. Drop in 8 balls at a time. Cook 3 minutes. Remove to a paper-towel-lined cookie sheet and keep warm in a 200° oven while frying the other two batches. Serve on cocktail picks or in sauce (see following recipe) in a chafing dish. Or place on a platter around a bowl of sauce. *Makes 24.*

Can be frozen without sauce. To reheat, place on cookie sheet and heat at 400° for about 10 minutes.

Sauce for Pork Balls

¾ cup Duck Sauce
2 teaspoons soy sauce

2 cloves garlic, minced (1 teaspoon)
½ teaspoon minced fresh ginger
2 tablespoons dry sherry
2 teaspoons chili sauce

SHANGHAI–NEW DELHI PORK BITES

These are handy to have in your repertoire, as they are much less time-consuming to make than meatballs, and once in the oven they require no watching. The dip takes less than 5 minutes to prepare.

1 pound boneless pork loin cut into 1-inch cubes

MARINADE
2 scallions, finely minced
2 cloves garlic, finely minced (1 teaspoon)
4 tablespoons dark soy sauce
2 tablespoons rice wine (*shao-hsing*) or dry sherry

Combine the marinade ingredients in a medium-sized bowl. Add the pork cubes and turn them to saturate them. Let them marinate for 2 hours at room temperature or overnight in the refrigerator. Preheat oven to 300°. Drain the pork and place the cubes on a shallow baking pan. Discard marinade. Bake for 1 hour. Serve on a platter, each pierced with a toothpick. In the center, place a small bowl of the following dip. (If you are serving these at a large party, it is convenient to put the pork in a chafing dish with the dip next to it on a warmer.) *Makes 20–24.*

Can be frozen. Freeze on a flat pan, then put into plastic bag and seal. To reheat, place on baking pan and bake in a preheated 400° oven for 20 minutes.

Dip for Pork Bites

4 tablespoons chopped chutney
4 tablespoons dark rum
½ cup unsweetened pineapple juice

Combine ingredients in a small saucepan, heat to boiling, and simmer 2 minutes.

This dip can be made in advance and refrigerated as much as 4 days, or can be frozen. *Makes about ¾ cup.*

CHINESE ROAST PORK STRIPS

Although most cooks have often made pork roasts, many people seem to think of the thin slices of Chinese-style roast pork as involving some inscrutable Oriental procedure. Actually, except for the marinating, these take very little time. They may be eaten warm or cold, but most people prefer them warm. I usually put them on a hot tray with a dip (see following recipe) in a small chafing dish.

> 2 pounds boneless pork loin, tenderloin, or boneless butt, cut into
>   strips about 6 inches long and 1½ inches in width and thickness
> ½ cup dark soy sauce
> 2 tablespoons rice wine (*shao-hsing*) or dry sherry
> ¼ cup honey
> ¼ cup hoisin sauce
> 2 cloves garlic, finely minced
> 2 tablespoons sugar
> 1 teaspoon Five-Spice Powder
> 2 teaspoons grated fresh ginger
> ¼ cup sesame oil
> ½ cup white corn syrup

Place the pork strips in a long glass dish. Combine all the remaining ingredients except the corn syrup, pour the mixture over the pork strips and marinate for 3 hours at room temperature or overnight in the refrigerator, turning them every half hour if possible. Preheat oven to 350°. Pour water into a roasting pan to a depth of about 1 inch and put a rack over it. Drain the pork strips, reserving the marinade. Put the strips on the rack and roast for ½ hour, then turn the strips, baste them with the marinade, and roast another ½ hour. At the end of 1 hour raise the oven temperature to 450° and roast another 15 minutes, turning and basting every 5 minutes. Pour the corn syrup into a platter, and as you remove the strips, dip them into the syrup, turning them several times to be sure they are well coated. Slice thin.

Pantry Shelf Red Dip

1 tablespoon chili sauce
3 tablespoons catchup
¼ cup peanut butter
¾ cup reserved marinade from pork

Combine all the ingredients in a saucepan and stir constantly while heating.

The strips and dip may both be made as much as 2 days in advance and reheated. To reheat the strips, wrap them in foil and bake in a preheated 350° oven for 15 minutes. Open the foil and bake another 5 minutes. *Makes about 32 slices.*

Can be frozen. When strips are cool, wrap them in heavy foil, seal with freezer tape, and freeze. To reheat, remove the tape and heat strips in the foil in a 375° oven for 30 minutes. Open the foil and bake another 10 minutes.

PORK OLÉ

These spicy pork bites (*carnitas*) were inspired by a tangy roast I savored in a flower-banked restaurant in Cuernavaca. They are assertive enough to be served without a dip, but the sauce (see following recipe) enhances their piquancy.

1 pound pork, boneless loin or very lean
   boneless butt, cut into 1-inch cubes
1 teaspoon salt
1½ teaspoons chili powder
1 teaspoon ground cumin
2 cloves garlic, put through press

Put the pork cubes on a piece of waxed paper and massage the salt, chili powder, cumin, and garlic juice into the meat. Let stand at room temperature for 1 hour. Preheat oven to 200°. Place the meat on a jelly-roll pan and bake for 1¼ hours. Raise oven heat to 300° and bake an additional 15 minutes. Drain on paper towels. Serve with toothpicks. Can be kept warm in a chafing dish. Serve the sauce in a bowl.

Both pork cubes and sauce may be made as much as 2 days ahead and reheated. Place the pork on the jelly-roll pan and bake in a preheated 350° oven for 8 minutes. Reheat the sauce slowly in a saucepan just until it reaches a boil. *Makes 20.*

Can be frozen. Freeze the cubes on a flat surface, then place in a plastic freezer bag and seal. Freeze the sauce in covered freezer container. To reheat, thaw cubes and sauce overnight in the refrigerator, bake cubes in a preheated 350° oven for 8 minutes, and heat sauce as above.

Cuernavaca Sauce

¼ cup vegetable oil
1 cup finely chopped onion
4 cloves garlic, finely minced (2 teaspoons)
2 cups tomato sauce
½ teaspoon salt
2 teaspoons chili powder
½ teaspoon ground cumin
½ teaspoon dried oregano

Heat the oil in a medium-sized saucepan and sauté the onion and garlic in it until wilted. Add the remaining ingredients and simmer, uncovered, for about 5 minutes.

BARBECUED BABY SPARERIBS

If a poll were taken to determine the all-time favorite finger food, barbecued ribs would probably be in the top ten. Cut into bite-sized morsels, they are easy to manage even if you are standing and using one hand to grasp a Martini. The spicy mixture that the ribs are tossed in eliminates the need for serving duck sauce and mustard.

1 small rack spareribs (about 2 pounds)
¼ cup cornstarch
1 cup oil for deep-frying
3 cloves garlic, minced (1½ teaspoons)
1 teaspoon minced fresh ginger
2 tablespoons Worcestershire sauce
2 tablespoons rice wine (*shao-hsing*) or dry sherry
¼ cup catchup
6 dashes Tabasco
1 teaspoon sugar
1 teaspoon sesame oil

Have the spareribs cut into individual ribs and then cut crosswise into 1½-inch pieces. Save the bony part for another use. Remove the thin film of skin on the back of the ribs. Put the cornstarch on a plate and turn the ribs in it to coat. In a skillet, heat the oil to 375° and fry the ribs in batches. Drain on paper towels. When all the ribs have been fried to a golden brown (about 8 minutes), pour off all but 1 teaspoon of oil. Add the garlic and ginger to the oil and sauté 1 minute. Add the remaining ingredients and stir until combined. Return the ribs to the pan and stir to coat them. Stir over medium heat, turning often, until they are heated through and slightly glazed. *Makes about 30.*

Can be frozen. Freeze on a flat pan, then put into plastic bag and seal. Thaw overnight in the refrigerator. Bake in a preheated 425° oven for 5 to 7 minutes.

BACON-WRAPPED CHICKEN LIVERS
(Rumaki)

I had written off this recipe as a cliché, but on a recent vacation in the British West Indies, every gathering featured two chafing dishes, one with cubes of native fried fish and the other with rumaki, which is the Polynesian version of bacon-wrapped chicken livers. I was intrigued, not so much at how fast they disappeared but by the number of guests who did not know how to make them. When making rumaki, use the leanest bacon you can find and partially cook it ahead. Put the slices on the rack of a baking pan and bake in a preheated 400° oven for about 10 minutes (the bacon will be cooked further).

While this is the most popular bacon-wrapped combination, the preparation varies: sometimes no marinade is used; sometimes only the liver, and sometimes the whole skewered tidbit, is marinated. The following is the version I find most successful. Other suggestions for bacon-wrapped tidbits follow.

12 chicken livers, cut in half

MARINADE
½ cup soy sauce
¼ cup dry sherry
4 teaspoons grated fresh ginger
2 tablespoons brown sugar
8 cloves garlic, minced (4 teaspoons)
12 slices bacon, cut in half and partly cooked
12 water chestnuts, cut in half

Wash and drain the chicken livers. Combine the marinade ingredients in a glass bowl and marinate the livers 1 hour. Drain thoroughly. Preheat oven to 400°. Wrap a half slice of bacon around a half chicken liver and a half water chestnut and secure with a wooden toothpick, inserting it through the lean streak of the bacon on both sides. Place on a rack on a baking pan and bake 10 to 15 minutes. Drain on paper towels for about a minute. These keep well in a chafing dish. If you are serving them on a platter, decorate the center with scallion fans interspersed with drained canned kumquats. These can be prepared a day in advance and refrigerated until you are ready to cook them. *Makes 24.*

Can be frozen. Bake only 15 minutes. Freeze on flat surface, then place in a plastic freezer bag and seal securely. To serve, preheat oven to 450°. Place the tidbits on a rack on a broiling pan and bake 15 minutes or until the bacon is brown and crisp. The next two recipes can be frozen in the same way.

Crab Balls in Bacon

1 6½-ounce can crabmeat
½ teaspoon dry mustard
2 teaspoons grated onion
½ teaspoon salt
1 tablespoon dry sherry
¼ cup fine dry bread crumbs
1 tablespoon finely chopped parsley
1 pound bacon slices, cut in half and partly cooked

Combine all ingredients except the bacon. Using a measuring teaspoon, form the mixture into tiny balls. Wrap each ball in a half slice of bacon. Proceed as in preceding recipe. *Makes about 48.*

Scallops in Bacon

6 tablespoons vegetable oil
3 tablespoons lemon juice
1 teaspoon salt
¼ teaspoon freshly ground pepper
1 clove garlic, minced (½ teaspoon)
2 tablespoons finely chopped parsley
2 tablespoons finely chopped chives
1 pound sea scallops
½ pound sliced bacon, slices cut in half and partly cooked

In a bowl, combine oil, lemon juice, salt, pepper, garlic, parsley, and chives. Add the scallops and marinate for 30 minutes at room temperature. Remove the scallops and dry on paper towels. Wrap a half slice of bacon around each scallop and bake as in Bacon-Wrapped Chicken Livers. *Makes about 24.*

Shrimp in Bacon

½ cup soy sauce
6 tablespoons bourbon
4 cloves garlic, chopped (2 teaspoons)
1 tablespoon sesame oil
1 tablespoon brown sugar
24 medium-sized shrimp, shelled and deveined
½ pound sliced bacon, cut in half and partly cooked

Combine the soy sauce, bourbon, garlic, sesame oil, and brown sugar in a glass bowl. Marinate the shrimp in this for 1 hour. Drain thoroughly. Wrap each shrimp in a half slice of bacon. Proceed as for Bacon-Wrapped Chicken Livers. *Makes 24.*

OTHER SUGGESTIONS FOR BACON-WRAPPED TIDBITS
Prepare as in main recipe.
Mussels or oysters marinated in lemon juice with a dash of Tabasco
Smoked mussels or smoked oysters
Cocktail franks or cocktail sausages, slit, with a small sliver of Cheddar cheese inserted; a tiny slice of gherkin can be added
Tiny meatballs or braunschweiger balls
Chicken-breast cubes and mushroom caps marinated in teriyaki sauce
Pitted dried prunes, plumped in boiling water, allowed to stand overnight, and then soaked in port wine for a few days; centers filled with a mixture of Cheddar cheese spread and chopped chutney or of Roquefort cheese and chopped pecans
Pitted ripe olives stuffed with Cheddar or Boursin cheese
Marinated artichoke hearts, or watermelon rind, or banana slices dipped in curry powder
Brazil nuts
Cocktail olives

BACON HUSH PUPPIES

Supposedly, hush puppies were so named because fishermen, while frying their early-morning catch, would throw bits of the batter into the pan and then feed them to the barking dogs to silence them—"hush, puppies."

    oil for deep frying
    1½ cups cornmeal
    ½ cup flour
    2 teaspoons salt
    ⅛ teaspoon cayenne powder
    2 tablespoons baking powder
    ½ teaspoon baking soda

1 egg, beaten
1½ cups buttermilk
6 tablespoons chopped onion
½ pound bacon (about 12 slices), baked on a broiling pan
    in a 400° oven for 20 minutes, then crumbled

Preheat the oil in a deep-fryer to 375°. Line two baking sheets with paper towels. Preheat oven to 250°. Combine all the ingredients and drop by half-teaspoonfuls into the hot fat. Cook, turning, until golden. Drain on paper towels. These may be kept warm for a few minutes in the oven.

Hush puppies can be made 1 or 2 days in advance and reheated. Place a wire rack over a jelly-roll pan and place the puppies on the rack. Bake in a preheated 425° oven for 8 minutes. *Makes 60.*

Can be frozen. Freeze in aluminum foil pans. Then cover with a plastic freezer bag and seal. Reheat, frozen, at 425° for 15 minutes.

NEW ENGLAND HUSH PUPPIES
Increase the cornmeal to 2 cups. Omit the bacon and add 4 8-ounce cans minced clams, thoroughly drained, 8 dashes Tabasco, and 2 teaspoons dill seed.

BONNIE EGGS

A traditional Scottish snack makes an unusual cocktail accompaniment.

1 pound bulk pork sausage
1 teaspoon onion juice
½ clove garlic, put through press
1 teaspoon dried basil
½ teaspoon dried thyme
4 eggs
½ cup fine dry bread crumbs
8 hard-cooked eggs, shelled
vegetable oil for deep-frying

In a large bowl, combine the sausage, onion juice, garlic, basil, and thyme. Beat the 4 eggs in a small bowl, then set aside. Spread the bread crumbs on waxed paper. Moisten your hands and put a portion of the sausage mixture into the palm of one hand. Flatten slightly with the other palm. Mold the mixture around each hard-cooked egg. Roll between palms to reshape. Dip the coated eggs into the beaten eggs and then roll in bread crumbs until completely coated. Place on another sheet of waxed paper. Refrigerate 1 hour or more. Heat the oil in a deep-fryer to 370°. Drop 2 coated eggs at a time into the oil and cook for 6 minutes. Remove with a slotted spoon to paper towels. Keep warm in a 200° oven while frying the remaining eggs. When serving hot, the following sauce enhances the flavor. These can be made a day in advance and reheated on a rack placed over a jelly-roll pan in a 450° oven for 5 minutes. They are also good cold. Cut into slices and place on melba toast spread with mustard-flavored butter, or cut into squares and serve with cocktail picks. *Makes 8.*

Sauce for Bonnie Eggs

  1 cup medium-thick White Sauce (below)
  1 tablespoon Escoffier Sauce Diable
  ½ teaspoon Dijon mustard

Combine all the ingredients in a saucepan and heat gently.

Medium-Thick White Sauce (Makes 1 cup)

  2 tablespoons butter or margarine
  2 tablespoons flour
  1 cup milk
  salt and freshly ground pepper

Melt the butter in a heavy saucepan over moderate heat, add the flour and stir with a wire whisk until it is well blended. Let the mixture simmer over low heat for two minutes, whisking constantly. Off the heat, gradually add the milk, stirring constantly. Return to the fire and whisk until the mixture comes to a boil. Season to taste with salt and pepper.

CHAFING-DISH HERO SANDWICHES

These always evoke happy memories of the Feast of San Gennaro held annually in the Little Italy section of lower New York. Make plenty—guests never seem to tire of fixing their own.

¾ cup olive oil
2 cups finely chopped onion
4 cloves garlic, finely minced (2 teaspoons)
2 pounds Italian frying peppers, cut into 1-inch squares
½ pound mushrooms, sliced
1½ teaspoons salt
¼ teaspoon crushed red pepper
1 teaspoon Italian herb seasoning
1½ pounds Italian sweet sausages, preferably
  a thin variety
white wine
1 8¾-ounce jar fire-roasted sweet peppers, washed,
  dried, and cut into slices 1 inch by ¾-inch
1 long, narrow loaf Italian or French bread
  (about 15 inches)

In a large heavy skillet, heat the olive oil. Add the onions, garlic, frying peppers, and mushrooms and sauté 10 minutes. Cover skillet and cook another 5 to 10 minutes, stirring occasionally. Add salt, red pepper, and herb seasoning. Place the sausages in another skillet and cover with water. Cover skillet; bring to a boil, lower heat, and simmer 5 minutes. Turn sausages and simmer 5 minutes more. Pour off water and cook the sausages slowly, turning to brown on all sides. Pour off fat as it accumulates. They should take about 20 to 30 minutes to cook through. Deglaze the pan with a little white wine just before removing sausages. Drain on paper towels. Slice into ½-inch pieces. Add the sausages and the roasted peppers to the onion-pepper mixture and cook just until the mixture is heated through. Pour into a chafing dish and have a basket of sliced Italian or French bread nearby so guests can make their own heroes. *Makes 15–20.*

Can be frozen. Freeze mixture in a freezer container. Defrost overnight in the refrigerator and reheat in a saucepan.

ITALIAN SAUSAGE ROLLS

4 tablespoons butter
½ pound Italian sweet sausages
2 tablespoons Vermouth
1 cup grated Parmesan cheese
1 teaspoon Italian herb seasoning
¼ teaspoon salt
⅛ teaspoon freshly ground black pepper
¼ teaspoon dried basil
8 slices firm white bread
4 tablespoons melted butter

Put the 4 tablespoons butter in a medium-sized bowl and allow to soften to room temperature. Prick the sausages in a few places on all sides. Place in a skillet, cover with water, and bring to a boil. Lower heat and simmer, covered, 10 minutes. Drain off the water and brown sausages, slowly pouring off the fat as it accumulates. When sausages are browned on all sides, add the Vermouth to the pan and raise heat. Cook for 2 minutes more. Drain on paper towels. When slightly cooled, cut into 3-inch slices. When the butter has softened, add the Parmesan cheese, herb seasoning, salt, pepper, and basil. Combine into a smooth paste. Preheat oven to 400°. Cut crusts off bread. With a rolling pin, flatten the slices slightly. Spread each slice with the cheese mixture, place a slice of sausage on top, and roll bread jelly-roll fashion. Place rolls, seam side down, on a greased baking sheet. Brush tops with the melted butter. Bake for about 12 minutes. Cut each roll in half. *Makes 16.*

Can be frozen. Before adding melted butter, freeze rolls seam side down on a flat surface. When ready to serve, brush with melted butter and bake in a preheated 400° oven for about 18 minutes.

SLIGHTLY POTTED COCKTAIL FRANKS

Here is an easy way to present cocktail frankfurters in a different dress with very little extra effort. They may be prepared 1 or 2 days in advance and reheated.

½ pound cocktail frankfurters, preferably
   Kosher, cut in half

SAUCE
½ cup bourbon
½ cup chili sauce
¼ cup dark brown sugar
2 teaspoons Dijon mustard
2 tablespoons tomato preserves

Combine sauce ingredients and bring to a boil. Simmer 5 minutes.
Add the frankfurters, cover, and simmer 15 minutes, stirring oc-
casionally. Transfer to a chafing dish and have toothpicks nearby.
Makes 36.

CHICKEN PUFFS

1 tablespoon butter
¼ cup finely minced mushrooms
1 clove garlic, put through press (¼ teaspoon)
¼ cup butter
½ cup chicken broth
¾ cup flour
2 eggs
1 cup finely minced cooked chicken
¼ cup finely chopped, toasted, blanched almonds
½ teaspoon salt
¼ teaspoon freshly ground black pepper
2 tablespoons chopped parsley
2 teaspoons onion juice
1 teaspoon dried tarragon
oil for deep frying

Melt the butter and sauté the mushrooms until they are browned
and most of the moisture has disappeared. Add the garlic for the
last minute. Lightly butter 2 baking sheets. Preheat oven to
450°. Place the butter and chicken broth in a saucepan and bring
to a boil over low heat. Off the heat, add the flour and stir vigorously. Return pan to low heat and beat until the mixture leaves

the sides of the pan and forms a ball. Cool for a few minutes.
Place mixture in the bowl of an electric mixer. Add the eggs, one
at a time, beating well after each addition. Fold in the chicken,
almonds, salt, pepper, parsley, onion juice, tarragon, and mushrooms. In a deep-fryer or electric skillet, heat the oil to 365°.
Drop in the mixture by teaspoonfuls, about 6 at a time, turning
the puffs to brown evenly. When they are golden, remove to paper
towels to drain. They may be kept warm on paper-towel-lined
pans in a 250° oven for 10 minutes.

These may be made a day in advance and reheated. To
heat, place a wire rack on a jelly-roll pan and place the puffs on
the rack. Bake in a preheated 425° oven for 8 minutes. *Makes
about 40.*

Can be frozen. Freeze puffs on a flat surface, then put in a
plastic bag and seal. Reheat as above but at 350° for 15 minutes.

CRUNCHY SOUTHERN
CHICKEN NUGGETS

    1 whole chicken breast, about 1 pound,
      skinned and boned
    1 egg white, beaten
    2 tablespoons cornstarch
    1 cup chopped pecans
    oil for deep-frying

    MARINADE
    ¼ cup bourbon
    1 teaspoon salt
    1 teaspoon sugar
    ½ teaspoon white pepper

Cut the chicken breast into 1-inch cubes. Combine marinade ingredients and place chicken cubes in the mixture, stirring until all
pieces are coated. Marinate 3 hours at room temperature or overnight in the refrigerator. Drain and dry the chicken pieces. Combine the egg white and cornstarch in a small bowl. Dip the pieces

into the coating, and then roll in the chopped pecans. Chill for 1 hour. Heat the oil in a deep-fryer at 350°. Fry the cubes for about 5 minutes. Drain on paper towels.

These may be made in advance and refrigerated. To reheat, preheat oven to 425°. Place a wire rack on a jelly-roll pan and place the cubes on the rack and heat for 8 to 10 minutes, or until hot. *Makes about 20.*

SWEET-AND-SOUR
MOCK CHICKEN DRUMSTICKS

Chinese cuisine is noted not only for its sophistication and almost infinite variety but also for its economy. So it is not surprising that the Chinese can transform a chicken wing into an exciting treat, whose origin usually mystifies people when they first meet it. The light crunchy batter used in this recipe was created by Florence Lin, a well-known Chinese cookbook author and teacher. Transforming chicken wings into drumsticks takes a little time and patience, but once you have done a few, the procedure will speed up.

12 chicken wings

MARINADE
1 cup light soy sauce
½ cup dry sherry or rice wine (*shao-hsing*)
4 cloves garlic, finely minced (2 tablespoons)
2 teaspoons grated fresh ginger
¼ teaspoon freshly ground pepper
4 scallions, finely minced
2 teaspoons sugar
2 teaspoons sesame oil

First prepare the chicken wings. Chop off the wing tips and discard. Chop the remaining sections of the wing apart at the joint. Start at the narrow end of the larger section and go toward the thicker part. With a boning knife, scrape the meat against the bone. Cut through the cartilage as you go. When about three-quarters of the bone is exposed, pull the meat over the end of the bone, like taking off a stocking. The meat is now on the outside and the skin on the inside. Smooth the meat with your fingers and you will have what looks like a chicken lollipop. Take the smaller section of the wing, the part with two bones, and chop the joint off each end. (A Chinese cleaver is excellent for this.) Starting at either end, again with a boning knife, loosen the skin and cartilage. As you proceed, the smaller bone will be easy to remove; simply twist it off. Work the rest of the meat off the main bone and shape it as with the larger half. You now have two miniature drumsticks from each wing.

Combine the marinade ingredients and then marinate chicken for 2 hours at room temperature or overnight in the refrigerator.

Drain the wings, reserving the marinade. Heat the oil in a deep-fryer to 375° and prepare the batter.

BATTER
1½ cups flour
½ cup cornstarch
4 teaspoons baking powder
about 1½ cups water
3 tablespoons hot oil from deep-fryer

Put the flour, cornstarch, and baking powder into a bowl. Gradually add water, stirring with a whisk to make a smooth medium-thick batter. Just before using, add the 3 tablespoons hot oil from the deep fryer. Coat each wing section with the batter and deep-fry in the hot oil about 4 to 5 minutes or until golden. Drain on paper towels. These can be kept warm for a few minutes in a 250° oven. Serve on a platter with a few scallion brushes as decoration and place a bowl of dip (see following recipe) in the center.

These can be made a day in advance and reheated. Place a wire rack on a jelly-roll pan and place the wings on the rack and heat in a preheated 425° oven for about 10 minutes. *Makes 24.*

Can be frozen. Both the wings and the dip can be frozen. Freeze wings on a flat surface, then place in a plastic bag and seal. Thaw overnight in the refrigerator and heat as above. Thaw the dip and reheat it slowly in a saucepan.

Dip for Mock Drumsticks

1 8-ounce can unsweetened, crushed pineapple
6 tablespoons reserved marinade
4 tablespoons rice wine vinegar
2 tablespoons catchup
2 tablespoons sugar
2 tablespoons rice wine (*shao-hsing*) or dry sherry
1 clove garlic, minced (½ teaspoon)
1 teaspoon grated fresh ginger
1 tablespoon cornstarch dissolved in 2 tablespoons water
1 teaspoon sesame seed oil

In a small saucepan, combine the pineapple, marinade, vinegar, catchup, sugar, wine, garlic, and ginger. Heat slowly to a boil, stirring to help dissolve the sugar. Stir the cornstarch-water mixture, lower the heat, and add to the saucepan, stirring constantly until sauce thickens. Just before removing from the heat, stir in the sesame oil.

Italian Mock Chicken Drumsticks

12 chicken wings
2 eggs, beaten
2 cloves garlic, put through press (½ teaspoon)
½ cup cornstarch
1 teaspoon baking powder
½ cup freshly grated Parmesan cheese
¼ cup Italian style seasoned bread crumbs
2 teaspoons salt
½ teaspoon freshly ground black pepper
4 teaspoons Italian herb seasoning
oil for deep frying

After preparing the chicken wings as for Sweet-and-Sour Drumsticks, combine the beaten eggs and the garlic in a shallow bowl. On a plate, combine the cornstarch, baking powder, Parmesan cheese, bread crumbs, salt, pepper, and Italian herb seasoning. Holding each wing by the exposed bone, dip it first in the egg mixture and then in the cornstarch-crumb mixture. Place them on a wire rack and refrigerate at least 1 hour. Heat the oil in a deep fryer to 350°. Fry wing sections a few at a time for about 4 to 5 minutes, turning once, until they are golden. Drain on paper towels. They may be kept warm in a 250° oven for a few minutes. Serve on a platter with chicory and Italian black olives in the center. *Makes 24.*

ORIENTAL HIGH FLYERS

A less time-consuming method of preparing chicken wings.

    12 chicken wings
    ½ cup soy sauce
    ¼ cup dry sherry
    ¼ cup brown sugar
    2 cloves garlic, crushed (1 teaspoon)
    2 teaspoons grated fresh ginger
    2 tablespoons lemon marmalade
    2 teaspoons grated orange rind

Cut off wing tips and separate each wing at the joint. Combine the remaining ingredients in a medium-sized glass bowl. Add the wings and stir to cover completely. Marinate for at least 4 hours at room temperature or overnight in the refrigerator. Turn wings in marinade three or four times. Preheat oven to 350°. Line a baking pan with foil and place wings on it. Brush with marinade, reserving rest of marinade. Bake for 40 minutes, brushing with reserved marinade every 10 minutes. Turn wings after 20 minutes. This is sticky finger food—provide plenty of paper napkins. *Makes 24 pieces.*

Can be frozen. See Sweet-and-Sour Drumsticks. Reheat on foil at 350° for 10 minutes, baste, turn, and bake 10 minutes more.

Hot Cheese
Hors d'Oeuvres

In most Western countries, in spite of the increase in "junk" foods, cheese remains the all-time snack staple. Served hot and embellished with other ingredients, it makes a satisfying main course and in smaller portions an ever-popular prelude to a heartier repast. The number of varieties is immense and still increasing. Supermarkets now stock cheese from many different countries, and Americans are no longer limited to processed concoctions. And the ways in which cheese can be served as a hot appetizer are almost endless.

In cooking with cheese, it is important to remember that unless the cheese is grated or shredded, you must use low heat or a double boiler to prevent the cheese from becoming stringy.

ALPINE BALLS

The ordinary Swiss cheese ball raised to a new peak by the addition of prosciutto.

5 ounces Swiss or Gruyère cheese, grated (1¼ cups)
1 tablespoon flour
pinch white pepper
¼ teaspoon salt
1½ teaspoons Worcestershire sauce
¼ pound finely chopped prosciutto
3 egg whites, stiffly beaten
⅓ cup fine dry bread crumbs
⅓ cup seasoned bread crumbs
oil for deep-frying

Combine the grated cheese with the flour, pepper, salt, Worcester-shire sauce, and prosciutto. Fold the stiffly beaten egg whites into the cheese mixture. Spread the bread crumbs on waxed paper. Using a measuring teaspoon, shape the mixture into balls about 1 inch in diameter. Roll the balls in the crumbs. Chill at least 1 hour. Pour oil into a deep-fryer or heavy saucepan to a depth of 2 inches and heat to 375°. Fry a few balls at a time for 1 minute or until golden brown. Remove with a slotted spoon and drain on paper towels. Serve hot. Decorate the serving platter with parsley, cherry tomatoes, and ripe olives.

These can be made in advance and reheated. Place on a wire rack on a baking sheet and heat in a 425° oven for about 8 minutes. *Makes 16.*

Can be frozen. Freeze on flat surface, then place in plastic bags and seal. Thaw overnight in refrigerator and reheat as above.

OLIVE-CHEESE BALLS

    3 tablespoons butter
    1 teaspoon dry mustard
    ¼ teaspoon salt
    ¼ teaspoon dried oregano
    1 cup coarsely grated sharp Cheddar cheese
        (¼ pound)
    ½ cup flour
    15 stuffed green jumbo olives

Cream the butter in an electric mixer. Add the mustard, salt, and oregano and beat until well blended. Beat in the grated cheese and then the flour. Drain the olives and pat dry. Wrap about a teaspoon of dough around each olive, rolling it smoothly between your palms. Place on a baking sheet and chill for at least 1 hour. Bake in a 400° oven for 15 minutes. *Makes 15.*

Warning: When first removed from oven, olives are too hot to handle; let them stand a few minutes before serving.

Can be frozen. Place unbaked balls on a flat surface. When

frozen, put them into freezer bags and seal. To serve, place on a baking sheet and thaw in refrigerator for about 4 hours. Bake as above.

POLISH-AMERICAN CHEESE BALLS
Omit the oregano and the olives. Add 1 teaspoon caraway seed and 2 ounces kielbasa, sliced ¼-inch thick, then each slice cut in half. Wrap a teaspoon of dough around each slice of kielbasa.

TEXAS CHEESE BALLS

> 5 ounces Vermont Cheddar cheese, grated (1¼ cups)
> 1 tablespoon flour
> 2 tablespoons finely chopped roasted and peeled
>   green chilies (available whole in cans)
> 2 tablespoons finely chopped ripe olives
> 3 egg whites, stiffly beaten
> ½ cup fine dry bread crumbs
> oil for deep-frying

Combine grated cheese, flour, chopped chilies, and chopped olives. Fold the beaten egg whites into the mixture. Spread the bread crumbs on waxed paper. Using a measuring teaspoon, shape the mixture into balls about 1 inch in diameter. Roll balls in the crumbs. Chill at least 1 hour. Heat oil in a deep-fryer to 375°. Fry for 1 minute or until golden. Drain on paper towels. Serve on a plate around a bunch of chicory decorated with pitted ripe olives filled with thin carrot or scallion strips.

These can be made in advance and reheated in a 425° oven on a wire rack placed on a jelly-roll pan. Bake about 8 minutes. *Makes 16.*

Can be frozen. Freeze on a flat surface, then place in plastic bag and seal. Thaw overnight in refrigerator and reheat as above.

CHEESE DOTS

¼ pound butter (1 stick), cold
¾ cup flour
¼ cup sour cream
2 cups grated Cheddar cheese
1 egg beaten with 1 tablespoon heavy cream
chopped toasted almonds or sliced Brazil nuts or
    salad seasoning

Cut the butter into the flour with a pastry blender or two dull knives, or use a food processor. Work until the butter is almost completely incorporated, using the tips of your fingers to complete the process. Stir in the sour cream and mix with a large spoon until thoroughly blended. Divide the dough in half and wrap parts in plastic wrap. Refrigerate 8 hours or overnight. Preheat oven to 350°. On a well-floured board, roll out half the dough into a rectangle 10 by 6 inches and about ⅛-inch thick. Sprinkle with ½ cup of the cheese. Fold the edges of the long sides over so they meet in the center. Reroll the pastry. Sprinkle with another ½ cup of cheese and fold the sides over again. Reroll into a 10- by 6-inch rectangle. Repeat with the other half of the dough and the remaining cup cheese. With a 1½-inch cookie cutter, cut circles of pastry. Place on a baking sheet lined with silicone-parchment paper. Brush the top of each with the egg-cream mixture and sprinkle with nuts or seasoning. Bake in a preheated 350° oven for 15 minutes. Cheese dots may be served hot or cold. *Makes about 48.*

Can be frozen. Reheat without thawing in a preheated 350° oven for 8 minutes.

DANISH SLICES

pastry for a 2-crust pie
½ teaspoon caraway seeds
2 cups crumbled Danish blue cheese (about ½ pound)
2 ounces cream cheese
2 egg yolks

2 tablespoons chopped chives
1 egg beaten with 1 tablespoon cream

Make your favorite pie crust, adding the caraway seeds. Refrigerate while making the filling. Crumble the blue cheese into the bowl of an electric mixer or food processor. Add the cream cheese. Let the cheeses soften to room temperature. Then cream the cheese and the egg yolks together until the mixture is smooth. Stir in the chives. Divide the pastry in half. Roll out each half into a rectangle 12 by 5 inches and about ⅛-inch thick. Spread ½ cup of the cheese mixture on each half of the pastry, to within ¼ inch of the edges. Roll up each half jelly-roll fashion. Seal the edges with part of the egg-cream mixture. Place the rolls on a baking sheet covered with silicone-parchment paper and chill 1 hour.

Preheat oven to 400°. Brush the top of each roll with the remaining egg-cream mixture. Cut rolls into slices ½-inch thick. Place the slices on the baking sheet. Bake at 400° for 10 minutes. Raise the temperature to 425° and bake 5 minutes longer. Serve warm. These can be made in advance and reheated at 375° for 5 minutes. *Makes 48.*

Can be frozen. Freeze cooked slices on aluminum foil trays. When frozen, wrap in plastic bags and seal. To serve, bake unthawed in a preheated 350° oven for 15 minutes.

GENOESE FRIED CHEESE STICKS

This is a simplified version of the famous *mozzarella en carozza*—mozzarella cheese sitting in a carriage. The "carriage" refers to the slices of bread between which the mozzarella is placed before being skewered and deep-fried. These are traditionally served with a hot anchovy sauce—delicious but rather messy as finger food. This adaptation requires only that your guests be supplied with paper napkins, not with bibs as well. The Pesto Mayonnaise (see recipe on page 22) would be a novel but happy accompaniment. If you cannot get really good fresh mozzarella, try this with Monterey Jack, which melts smoothly and has the proper tang.

1 pound mozzarella or Monterey Jack cheese
½ teaspoon salt
1 teaspoon Italian herb seasoning
½ cup flour
2 eggs, beaten
1 cup bread crumbs
½ cup olive oil

Cut the cheese into sticks about 3 inches long, ¼-inch thick, and ½-inch wide. On a sheet of waxed paper, combine the bread crumbs with the salt and herb seasoning. Dip each slice of cheese into the flour, then into the eggs, and then into the bread crumbs. (If you can refrigerate these for an hour or two, the coating will adhere better.) In a large, heavy skillet, heat the olive oil until it is almost boiling. Sauté the cheese sticks in the hot oil, turning every few seconds for about 2 minutes or until they are golden. Drain on paper towels and serve at once, if possible. Place on a platter with a bowl of Pesto Mayonnaise (see index) in the center. *Makes about 48.*

FRIED RICE BALLS
(Suppli al Telefono)

This snack is especially popular in northern Italy, where rice is served more often than pastas. Its Italian name comes from the fact that when you bite into one the melted cheese comes out in strings like telephone wires. Be careful to enclose the cheese completely or the "wires" will be lost in the cooking.

2 cups cooked rice, lukewarm
¼ cup grated Parmesan cheese
1 tablespoon finely chopped parsley
1 egg, beaten
⅛ teaspoon freshly ground pepper
¼ teaspoon freshly grated nutmeg
¼ pound prosciutto, finely chopped
¼ pound mozzarella cheese, cut into ½-inch cubes
½ cup flour

2 eggs, beaten with 1 teaspoon salt
¾ cup fine dry bread crumbs
oil for deep-frying

Combine the rice, Parmesan cheese, chopped parsley, the 1 beaten egg, pepper, nutmeg, and prosciutto. Place a tablespoon of the rice mixture in the palm of your hand and put a cube of mozzarella in the center. Place another tablespoon of the rice mixture on top, press together, and roll to form a ball. Roll immediately in the flour, dip in the beaten eggs, and roll in the bread crumbs. Repeat with the rest of the rice mixture. Refrigerate for at least 1 hour. Preheat oven to 250°. Heat the oil in a deep-fryer to 365°. Fry a few balls at a time for about 4 minutes or until golden. Drain on paper towels. As they are cooked, place the balls in the oven on a jelly-roll pan lined with paper towels until all are cooked. Serve on a tray with a tomato rose surrounded by curly parsley in the center.

These may be made a day ahead. To reheat, remove from refrigerator and let come to room temperature. Place a rack on a jelly-roll pan, and put the cooked balls on the paper. Reheat in a 425° oven for 15 minutes. *Makes 14–16.*

Can be frozen. Freeze on a flat surface, then place in a plastic freezer bag, and seal securely. Thaw overnight in the refrigerator and reheat as above.

MORTADELLA-STUFFED RICE BALLS

Omit the prosciutto from the rice mixture and add ½ teaspoon salt. Proceed as in preceding recipe, but omit the mozzarella and use ⅛ pound mortadella, cut in ½-inch cubes, and 2 ounces Bel Paese cheese, shredded, placing a mortadella cube and a pinch of Bel Paese in the center of each ball.

Filled
Pastries

There are few cocktail accompaniments as elegant as tiny piping-hot filled pastries. While these impressive morsels involve more work than a dip, they may be made at your leisure, some even a month or two in advance, and stored in the freezer. They can be the hub of the hors d'oeuvres for a long-planned extra-special party or they can be whipped out to serve unexpected guests. Once you have made a few of them, you will soon be inventing your own fillings.

If you are serving dinner afterward, don't present too many pastries. And if it is not feasible to pass the pastries around, set up a hot tray from which your guests can pick them up. If you serve more than one hot pastry, choose contrasting types of pastries and fillings. I have not included any yeast-based pastries, because I prefer cream-cheese- or sour-cream-based doughs, which produce as light and flaky a base as you could desire. If you do not want to make your own puff pastry, commercial puff pastry in sheets or shells from the freezer sections of supermarkets make a more than adequate substitute. You need only defrost them partly and roll them out. Or use Quick Puff Pastry (see index).

Other recipes in this book can be adapted for filling pastry.

Stuffed
Breads

Ideally these stuffed breads should be made with the thin loaves of French bread that are now being flown regularly to this country. But as these loaves are not available everywhere, the recipes have been adapted for brown-and-serve rolls.

SMALL STUFFED ROLLS

Use 3½- by 1¾-inch rolls. Bake the desired number of rolls according to package directions. Then make filling or fillings (quantities in filling recipes are for 1 roll). Cut off the ends of each roll, and carefully scoop out most of the center, leaving a shell about ¼ inch thick. (You can freeze the crumbs for other uses.) Stand one end of the roll on a piece of foil and stuff the mixture into the shell, pushing it down to the bottom. Do not try to force in too much filling or you may crack the crust. Wrap each filled shell securely in foil and refrigerate for at least 4 hours. When ready to serve, cut each roll into 1-inch slices. Arrange on a platter in concentric rings with olives or gherkins and a few radish roses in the center.

Hammy Danish Filling

1 ounce Danish blue cheese
1 ounce cream cheese
2 ounces chopped ham

1 tablespoon chopped parsley
1 tablespoon chopped chives
1½ tablespoons chopped fresh dill
1½ teaspoons cognac

Let cheese soften to room temperature. Add the remaining ingredients and combine until smooth.

Nutty Devilish Ham Filling

2¼ ounce Camembert cheese
4 tablespoons butter
2 tablespoons chopped walnuts
3 tablespoons Smithfield deviled ham
3 tablespoons minced sweet gherkins

Let cheese and butter soften to room temperature, then add the remaining ingredients and mix until smooth.

Liverwurst Filling

2 ounces liverwurst
2 ounces grated Muenster cheese
1½ teaspoon finely minced onion
½ teaspoon German mustard
1½ teaspoons chopped crisp bacon
2 tablespoons chopped pimiento-stuffed olives
¾ teaspoon Escoffier Sauce Diable

Using a large spoon, combine all the ingredients in a bowl.

WESTPHALIAN HAM ROLL

1 6-by-2½-inch roll
3 tablespoons butter, softened
¼ pound Camembert, rind removed
½ teaspoon dry mustard
2 tablespoons chopped toasted almonds
3 slices Westphalian ham

Cut roll in half lengthwise and cut off ends. Scoop out most of the soft center. Spread 1½ teaspoon of butter on each half. Combine the remaining 2 tablespoons butter with the Camembert, dry mustard, and chopped nuts. Place a slice of ham on each buttered half roll. Cover each slice with half the cheese mixture. Place the third slice of ham on top of one half roll. Put halves together and wrap securely in foil. Refrigerate at least 4 hours or up to 2 days. To serve, cut into ½-inch slices. *Makes about 10 slices.*

Can be frozen. Thaw overnight in refrigerator.

Popovers

Although many people are awed by popovers, they are one of the easiest of breads. Made in miniature and filled with almost any piquant mixture, they are a novel addition to the hors d'oeuvre table.

MINI-POPOVERS

½ cup sifted flour
¼ teaspoon salt
1 large egg
½ cup milk
1½ teaspoons melted butter

Preheat oven to 400°. Grease 16 tiny tart pans (1¾ inches wide and 1 inch deep). Put all the ingredients into a blender and blend at high speed for about 20 seconds, scraping down any flour that sticks to the sides. Fill the greased pans to about half their depth. Bake for 20 minutes. Do not open the oven door during this period. Turn the popovers out on a rack and cool a few minutes. Slit each on the side and stuff with one of the following fillings. Reheat in 400° oven for about 5 minutes. These can be made in the morning; slit them but do not fill until just before reheating. If you have any left over they can be frozen, but when reheated they will be a little too crusty and firm to rank as real popovers. To serve frozen filled popovers, put them on a pan, cover them lightly with foil, and bake in a preheated 400° oven for 20 minutes. *Makes 16.*

Chicken Filling

2 tablespoons butter
1 shallot, minced (1 teaspoon)
1 clove garlic, finely minced (½ teaspoon)
¼ pound mushrooms, finely minced
1 tablespoon flour
⅓ cup chicken stock
about ½ teaspoon salt (depending on the
　　saltiness of the stock)
dash Tabasco
1 egg yolk, beaten
¼ cup heavy cream
1 tablespoon dry sherry
1 teaspoon dried tarragon
½ cup chopped cooked chicken

In a small saucepan, melt the butter. Add the shallots, sauté 1 minute, and add the garlic and mushrooms. Sauté for 5 minutes. Add the flour and stir with a whisk for about 3 minutes. Add the chicken stock and whisk over medium heat until the sauce thickens. Add the salt and Tabasco. Combine the egg yolk and cream in a small bowl. Add a bit of the hot sauce to the yolk mixture and stir well. Add all the yolk mixture to the sauce. Add the sherry and heat. Remove from heat and add the tarragon and chopped chicken. *Fills about 16.*

Clam Filling

2 8-ounce cans minced clams, drained
2 3-ounce packages cream cheese with chives
4 cloves garlic, put through press (1 teaspoon)
½ teaspoon salt
4 dashes Tabasco sauce
2½ teaspoons Worcestershire sauce
2 teaspoons lemon juice
2 teaspoons grated onion
2 teaspoons finely chopped parsley
4 teaspoons finely chopped chives

Combine all the ingredients and fill the slit popovers. *Fills about 16.*

Sausage Stuffing

½ pound pork sausage
¼ cup chopped onion
4 cloves garlic, finely chopped (2 teaspoons)
½ beaten egg *
¼ teaspoon dried sage
¾ teaspoon crushed dried thyme
¼ cup grated sharp Cheddar cheese

Remove the sausage from the casing and sauté in a skillet until brown. Remove with a slotted spoon and drain on paper towels. Drain off all but 1 tablespoon of the fat from the skillet and sauté the onion until golden. Add the garlic and sauté another minute. Put the beaten half egg into a medium-sized bowl and add the sausage mixture, sage, thyme, and grated cheese. Mix well. *Fills 16.*

* To measure half an egg, beat 1 egg in a measuring cup and pour off half. An average large egg will be about ¼ cup.

Crêpes

Crêpes are more often served as a sit-down first course at an elegant dinner or as the main course at a special brunch or luncheon. However, as appetizers they provide a perfect carrier for many piquant fillings, especially when made in a bite-sized version.

I had not realized that crêpes were considered difficult to make until the recent proliferation of expensive automatic machines for the purpose. Their reputation for being a tricky creation, in the same category as a soufflé, may perhaps derive from their French name, but other cultures have their own versions: Italian *cannelloni*, Jewish blintz, Russian *blini*, Scandinavian *plättar*, and Chinese egg roll and spring roll. Actually there is no mystery to making crêpes, and they may be made as long as 2 days in advance if securely wrapped and refrigerated and, if packaged properly, may be frozen for months; in many instances, even frozen filled. Regular-sized crêpes may be cut into slices and served as finger food, but tiny crêpes ("crêpettes") make a more attractive presentation.

BASIC RECIPE FOR CRÊPETTES

These are most easily made in a Swedish pancake pan, which is heavy cast iron and has seven 3-inch depressions.

BATTER
⅓ cup water
⅓ cup milk

182

1 egg
½ cup sifted flour
¼ teaspoon salt
1 tablespoon melted butter

Note: For herbed batter, add 1 teaspoon each of chopped chives, chopped fresh dill, and chopped parsley.

If you are using a blender, put all the ingredients into the container and blend 1 minute. Stop the machine and with a rubber spatula scrape down any flour clinging to the sides of the jar. Blend another minute. (If you want herbed batter, stir in herbs at this point.) If you are making these by hand, beat the egg with a rotary beater or a whisk and then beat in the rest of the ingredients (including the herbs, if used). Pour the batter into a bowl, cover with plastic wrap, and let sit at room temperature for 1 hour or refrigerate overnight.

To cook the crêpettes melt about 2 tablespoons butter. Place the pancake pan over moderate heat for about 2 minutes. Lightly brush each depression with melted butter. It is not necessary to re-butter for each use. Remove the pan from the heat and quickly ladle 2 teaspoons batter into each depression. Tilt the pan in all directions so that the batter covers the depressions. Return the pan to the heat and cook for about 1 minute or until bubbles appear and the bottom is lightly browned. With a narrow spatula, flip crêpettes over and cook the other side for about 30 seconds. Turn out on a plate. The second side will be a bit mottled; it is often referred to as the nonpublic side, since it is the surface that is spread with the filling. If you are making the crêpes in advance, place waxed paper under each as you take it from the pan.

Fillings for crêpes may be any creamed or curried meat or fish mixture, vegetable purées, pâtés, cheese mixtures, caviar mixed with grated onion and sour cream (easy *blini*), or the Greek fish-roe spread, *tarama*. The following fillings are among those I have found to be favorites. Some are a bit more time-consuming than others. *Makes about 32.*

Can be frozen. Wrap each stack of 8 to 10 in foil and then

tightly seal in a freezer bag. They will keep for about 4 months. Defrost in the refrigerator overnight or for a few hours at room temperature. Be sure they are thoroughly defrosted; frozen crêpes are brittle and break easily.

Smoked Salmon Filling

Use herbed batter.

> 6 ounces whipped cream cheese
> ¼ pound smoked salmon, finely minced
> 2 tablespoons minced fresh dill
> 1 tablespoon grated onion

Combine all the ingredients. Put about 1½ teaspoons of the filling in the center of each crêpe, on the nonpublic side. Fold the sides up securely. These can be served cold or placed on a greased pan and heated in a 425° oven for 6–8 minutes. *Fills 32.*

Anchovy Filling

Use herbed butter.

> 6 ounces whipped cream cheese
> 1 tablespoon lemon juice
> 1 tablespoon anchovy paste
> 1 tablespoon grated onion
> 3 tablespoons minced fresh dill

Combine all the ingredients. Fill as above. Serve cold. *Fills about 20.*

Ham Filling

> ¼ pound ground ham
> 2 ounces Gruyère cheese, grated (½ cup)
> ¼ cup finely chopped scallions
> 4 ounces whipped cream cheese
> 1 teaspoon Dijon mustard
> 2 dashes Tabasco
> 2 teaspoons finely chopped parsley
> ½ teaspoon dried tarragon

Combine all the ingredients. Fill as above. Heat on a greased pan in a 425° oven for 6–8 minutes. Serve hot. *Fills about 32.*

Shrimp Filling

Use herbed batter.

SAUCE
2 tablespoons butter
2 tablespoons flour
⅔ cup clam broth

Melt the butter in a small heavy saucepan and stir in the flour. Whisk constantly over medium heat for 2 minutes. Add the clam broth and continue to whisk until the sauce thickens and bubbles. Remove from the heat and reserve.

SHRIMP MIXTURE
2 teaspoons chopped shallots
2 cloves garlic, finely chopped (1 teaspoon)
2 teaspoons butter
½ pound cooked shrimp, coarsely chopped
½ teaspoon salt
dash Tabasco
2 tablespoons finely chopped fresh dill
1 teaspoon lemon juice

Sauté the shallots and garlic in the butter for about 3 minutes. Add the remaining ingredients. Fold the mixture into the sauce. Fill and heat as above. *Fills about 32.*

CRÊPETTES WITH CHEESE

Crêpettes can form the base for a variation of the ever-popular *mozarella en carozza.* Make them with herbed batter. On each, place a piece of mozzarella about 2¼ inches long, ¼ inch wide, and ¼ inch thick. On top of this, spread about ⅛ teaspoon anchovy paste, sprinkle with freshly ground pepper, and roll. Serve hot.

If you have crêpettes already made in the refrigerator or freezer, bring to room temperature, place a small stick of Gruyère sharp Cheddar in the center of each, and roll up. Heat on a greased pan in a 425° oven for 6–8 minutes. Serve hot.

PIZZA CRÊPETTES

Julia Child revolutionized my approach to crêpes when she produced on her television program a cake made by layering crêpes with various fillings between the layers. Tiny crêpes lend themselves to this treatment, but for serving with cocktails it is impractical to build too high a tower. The only rule for the fillings is that they be compatible in flavor. Although this recipe might be frowned upon in Naples, it is much favored here.

> fillings (recipes follow)
> 8 teaspoons freshly grated Parmesan cheese
> 8 teaspoons melted butter

Prepare 2 batches of crêpettes according to the preceding basic recipe. Then make the fillings. Preheat oven to 400°. Grease a shallow baking pan large enough to hold 16 crêpettes. Put one crêpette on the pan and cover it with sausage filling. Place another on top and spread with spinach filling. Cover this with a third, spreading this with mushroom filling. Cover with a fourth crêpette. Continue until you have made 16 stacks of four crêpettes each. Sprinkle ½ teaspoon Parmesan cheese on top of each and pour ½ teaspoon melted butter over. Bake 10 minutes. With a small spatula, place 1 stack on each plate. Serve with small forks. *Makes 16 stacks of crêpettes.*

Can be frozen. Freeze on an aluminum tray, then seal securely in a plastic freezer bag. To serve, heat on a greased pan in a 400° oven for 30 minutes.

Sausage Filling

> ¼ pound sweet Italian sausage (usually 1 link)
> 1 tablespoon olive oil
> ½ cup finely chopped onion

1 clove garlic, finely chopped (½ teaspoon)
¾ cup tomato sauce
½ teaspoon Italian herb seasoning
1 tablespoon freshly grated Parmesan cheese

Prick the sausage in several places with a fork. Put in a small skillet with water to cover. Poach, covered, for about 6 minutes, turning once. Pour off the water and fry slowly for about 15 to 20 minutes until it is nicely browned and no longer pink inside. Remove and drain on paper towels. In the oil, sauté the onion until golden. Add the garlic and cook another 2 minutes. Finely chop the cooked sausage. Put into a bowl, add the onion and garlic and remaining ingredients, and stir to mix. Set aside.

Spinach Filling

4 teaspoons chopped shallots
2 teaspoons olive oil
½ cup chopped cooked spinach
3 tablespoons shredded mozzarella cheese
2 tablespoons whipped cream cheese
2 tablespoons ricotta cheese
generous ¼ teaspoon salt
pinch pepper
a few grates nutmeg
1 tablespoon grated Parmesan cheese
⅓ beaten egg

Cook the shallots in the olive oil for 3 minutes. Add all other ingredients except the egg and stir just until the cheeses melt. Cool a few minutes. Beat an egg in a measuring cup and stir a third of it into the mixture. Set aside.

Mushroom Filling

½ cup finely chopped shallots
6 tablespoons olive oil
4 cloves garlic, finely chopped (2 teaspoons)
1 pound mushrooms, finely minced
½ cup Italian Mornay sauce (recipe follows)
4 teaspoons finely chopped parsley

Sauté the shallots in the oil for about 3 minutes. Add the garlic and mushrooms and sauté another 8 minutes. Meanwhile make the Mornay Sauce. Remove mushroom mixture from heat and add the Sauce and parsley.

ITALIAN MORNAY SAUCE
1 tablespoon butter
1 tablespoon flour
½ cup milk
¼ teaspoon salt
pinch white pepper
a few grates nutmeg
2 tablespoons shredded mozzarella cheese
6 teaspoons grated Parmesan cheese

Melt the butter in a small, heavy saucepan and stir in the flour. Whisk constantly over medium heat for 2 minutes. Add the milk and continue to whisk until the sauce thickens and bubbles. Add the remaining ingredients. Stir just until the cheeses melt.

Chinese
Spring Rolls

Most people are familiar with Chinese egg rolls—unfortunately too often soggy cylinders. However, the egg roll has a delicate, flaky cousin—the spring roll, said to have acquired its name because it was offered to those who came calling at New Year's, the beginning of spring for the Chinese. While egg rolls have egg in the batter, spring-roll wrappers are a mixture of flour and water and provide a lighter skin. However, they are more difficult to make and handle than egg-roll wrappers, and even Chinese cooks usually purchase them. At the time of the Chinese New Year many supermarkets now stock these wrappers, as well as many Chinese vegetables. As the wrappers freeze very well, it is a good idea to stock up. Filled and fried spring rolls also can be stored in the freezer. Fillings can be meat, seafood, vegetables, or combinations of these.

PORK-AND-SHRIMP FILLING

6 large dried Chinese mushrooms
½ pound ground pork
2 tablespoons plus 2 teaspoons cornstarch
2 tablespoons plus 1 teaspoon dark soy sauce
½ pound shrimp, shelled and deveined
4 teaspoons rice wine (*shao-hsing*) or dry sherry
2 teaspoons salt
¼ teaspoon monosodium glutamate (optional)
6 tablespoons peanut oil
2 cloves garlic, finely chopped (1 teaspoon)
1 teaspoon finely chopped fresh ginger
1 cup finely chopped celery
2 cups shredded Chinese celery cabbage
½ cup shredded bamboo shoots
½ cup chopped scallions
½ cup finely diced water chestnuts
½ pound bean sprouts, preferably fresh,
   washed and drained
1 teaspoon sugar
2 teaspoons sesame oil
30 Shanghai spring-roll wrappers
2 eggs, beaten
oil for deep-frying

Soak the mushrooms in very hot water for 30 minutes. Drain them, reserving 3 tablespoons of the soaking liquid, squeeze them, and dry them on paper towels to remove as much of the liquid as possible. Cut off the tough stems and shred the mushrooms. While the mushrooms are soaking, combine the ground pork in a bowl with 1 teaspoon of the cornstarch and 1 teaspoon of the soy sauce. Mix well with your fingers. Dice the shrimp and place them in another bowl, adding 2 teaspoons of the wine or sherry, 1 teaspoon of the cornstarch, ½ teaspoon of the salt, and the monosodium glutamate (if used). Mix with your fingers—your most useful kitchen utensil. Set both of these bowls aside.

Meanwhile chop or shred the remaining ingredients as indicated. Combine the remaining 2 tablespoons of cornstarch with the reserved mushroom-soaking liquid. Heat a wok or large skillet, pour in 2 tablespoons of the peanut oil, and heat. Add the ground pork and stir constantly until the meat separates and loses its pink color. Add the shrimp mixture and stir constantly until the shrimp turn pink. With a slotted spoon, remove the pork and shrimp. Add the remaining 4 tablespoons peanut oil to the wok and put in the chopped garlic and ginger. Cook for a minute until they flavor the oil. Add the mushrooms and stir them to coat them with the oil. Add the celery, cabbage, and bamboo shoots, and stir constantly for about 4 minutes, until the cabbage wilts. Add the scallions, water chestnuts, and bean sprouts. Stir quickly and sprinkle in 2 teaspoons wine or sherry, 2 tablespoons soy sauce, 1 teaspoon sugar, and 1½ teaspoon salt. Stir again quickly so the seasonings can penetrate the mixture. Return the pork and shrimp to the pan and add the 2 teaspoons of sesame oil. Quickly stir again. Stir the cornstarch-mushroom liquid again to be sure the cornstarch is thoroughly dissolved, and add to the pan. Stir over high heat until the liquid thickens. Place the mixture in a colander and drain over a plate. Cool before using. If you are not filling the wrappers immediately, refrigerate the filling, covered, overnight.

If the wrappers were frozen, defrost them in the refrigerator overnight. When using them, cover them with a damp cloth, as they dry out very quickly. On your work counter, place a large baking sheet, the beaten eggs, a pastry brush, the filling, and the wrappers. Take out one wrapper at a time and place it on the counter with one point facing you. Place a generous 2 tablespoons of the filling near this lower corner but not too near the edges. Using your fingers, roll up the wrapper once, tucking in the point to enclose the filling. Brush the right and left sides of the wrapper with beaten egg, fold over the sides envelope-fashion, and press to seal. Continue to roll the wrapping around the enclosed filling until you have a neat cylinder. Press the top corner firmly to be sure it adheres, and place the roll, seam side down, on the baking sheet. Fill the remaining wrappers in the same way. If you do not plan to fry them immediately, cover with plastic wrap and refrigerate.

Heat the oil in a deep-fryer to 365° and fry a few rolls at a time, turning them to brown evenly. When they are golden, in about 4 to 5 minutes, remove with a slotted spoon and drain on paper towels. Keep warm on paper towels in a 250° oven until you have fried all you intend to serve.

As a cocktail hors d'oeuvre, cut each roll with a serrated knife into thirds. Serve with Duck Sauce or Chinese mustard. (To make your own Chinese mustard, slowly mix dry mustard with about an equal amount of boiling water and a pinch of salt. Let stand about ½ hour before using. Do not make more than you expect to use at one time.)

The rolls may be fried the day before and reheated. Place a wire rack on a baking pan and put the rolls on the rack and bake in a preheated 425° oven for 7 minutes. *Makes 30.*

Can be frozen. Place cooked rolls on foil baking tray and freeze; then place in large plastic bag and seal. Place unthawed rolls on a rack on a jelly-roll pan and heat in a 375° oven for 20–25 minutes.

Turnovers

Almost every nationality has its own version of turnovers—the English, Cornish pastries, the Latin Americans, *empanadas*; the Italians, *calzone*; the Chinese, *won ton*. The Russians rightly pride themselves on their *piroshki*—flaky boat-shaped pastries with a variety of fillings that are an integral part of a Russian hors d'oeuvre table and are often served as an accompaniment to soup. You can use Cream-Cheese Pastry (recipe follows), Quick Puff Pastry (see index), or frozen puff pastry.

BASIC TURNOVER RECIPE

Use Cream-Cheese Pastry.

Cream-Cheese Pastry

½ pound butter (2 sticks)
8 ounces cream cheese
1 teaspoon salt
2 cups flour

1 egg beaten with 1 tablespoon water
1 egg yolk, beaten with 2 teaspoons heavy cream

Bring the butter and cheese to room temperature. Beat together with the salt in an electric mixer or food processor until completely smooth and blended. Work in the flour to form a smooth dough, using a spatula, fork, or your fingertips. Flatten the dough on waxed paper to form an 8- by 6-inch rectangle. Wrap the waxed paper around the dough and cover with foil. Refrigerate overnight.

Remove dough from refrigerator 15 minutes before rolling out. Divide the dough in half and put half in the refrigerator. Roll the other half into a rectangle ⅛-inch thick. Fold over itself in thirds, roll again, fold over itself again, and roll into a 10-inch square. Cut into 3-inch rounds. Stack all the trimmings in layers; don't wad them up. Reroll until all the dough is used. Put ½ teaspoon of the selected filling in the center of each round; moisten the edges with a pastry brush dipped in the egg beaten with water and fold together over the filling. Press the edges with the floured tines of a fork to seal. Place pastries seam side up on an ungreased baking sheet. Flatten slightly and pinch the tips into an oval shape with pointed ends. Chill 1 hour. Brush the tops of the pastry with the egg yolk beaten with cream. Bake in a 350° oven for 30–35 minutes. *Makes about 50.*

Can be frozen. If turnovers are to be frozen, bake only 25 minutes. Freeze on aluminum foil trays, then cover with plastic wrap and seal. Reheat at 425° for about 15 minutes.

Beef-Dill Filling

2 tablespoons butter
½ cup minced onion
½ pound lean ground round beef
1 tablespoon flour
½ slightly beaten egg (see page 000)
2 teaspoons beef broth
¾ teaspoon salt
¼ teaspoon pepper
1 clove garlic, finely chopped (½ teaspoon)
5 tablespoons chopped fresh dill, including stems
   (for extra flavor)
½ cup cooked rice

In a medium-sized skillet, melt the butter and sauté the onion 5 minutes. Add the meat and keep tossing together with a fork until all signs of red have disappeared from the meat. Sprinkle with the flour, stir in, and add the egg and beef broth. Cook until thickened. Add the seasonings and rice. Combine well. *Fills about 50.*

Ham-Bacon-Cheese Filling

2 tablespoons butter
½ cup finely chopped onion
6 ounces cooked ham, finely chopped (1½ cups)
2 cups grated Cheddar cheese (½ pound)
1 hard-cooked egg, chopped
¼ cup crumbled cooked bacon
2 tablespoons mayonnaise
2 tablespoons chopped chives
¼ teaspoon salt

In a small skillet, melt the butter and sauté the onion until golden. Add the ham and sauté a few minutes more. Let cool. Stir in the cheese. Combine the egg, bacon, mayonnaise, chives, and salt. Add to the cooled mixture and stir well. *Fills about 50.*

TONGUE-FILLED TURNOVERS

Make these with so-called Quick Puff Pastry.

Quick Puff Pastry

½ pound butter (2 sticks)
1½ cups flour
pinch salt
½ cup sour cream
1 egg, beaten
1 egg yolk beaten with 2 teaspoons heavy cream

In a large mixing bowl of an electric mixer, cut the butter into the flour. Wrap a towel around the lip of the bowl to prevent spillage. Beat the mixture at low speed. Add the salt and sour cream and continue to beat until incorporated. Divide the dough in half and wrap halves in foil. Refrigerate 8 hours or overnight.

FILLING
2 tablespoons butter
½ cup chopped onion
1½ cups finely chopped pickled tongue, cooked
½ teaspoon Dijon mustard
1 hard-cooked egg, finely chopped
1 tablespoon chopped chives
1 tablespoon chopped parsley
¼ teaspoon salt
⅛ teaspoon freshly ground black pepper
2 tablespoons sour cream
1 teaspoon Worcestershire sauce

Melt the butter and sauté the onion until tender but not brown. Add the tongue and cook another minute. Off the heat, mix in the rest of the ingredients. Let cool.

Remove the dough from the refrigerator, roll out each half on a floured board to ⅛-inch thickness. Cut into 3-inch rounds. Put about ½ teaspoon of the filling in the center of each round; moisten the edges with the beaten egg and fold over the filling. Press the edges with the floured tines of a fork to seal. Set the pastries seam side up on an ungreased baking sheet. Flatten slightly and pinch the edges to create a boat shape. Chill 1 hour. Brush the tops with the egg yolk beaten with the cream. Bake in a 350° oven about 30 minutes. *Makes 36.*

Can be frozen. Freeze on foil pans, then put into plastic bags and seal. To serve, bake in a 425° oven for 15 minutes.

AMERICANIZED ITALIAN TURNOVERS
(Calzone)

Quick Puff Pastry (see preceding recipe).

Make the pastry as directed and refrigerate 8 hours or overnight. Make the filling just before using it.

FILLING
2 tablespoons butter
2 tablespoons finely chopped onion
½ pound ground beef
2 cloves garlic crushed in ½ teaspoon salt
2 teaspoons red wine
½ cup finely grated Parmesan cheese
¼ teaspoon freshly ground black pepper
1 teaspoon Italian herb seasoning
2 teaspoons finely chopped parsley
1 tablespoon seasoned bread crumbs
1 egg, lightly beaten
1 teaspoon heavy cream

In a medium-sized skillet, melt the butter. Sauté the onion until translucent. Add the meat and break up with a fork as it cooks. Cook until the meat loses its red color. Add the garlic-salt paste, the wine, cheese, pepper, and Italian herb seasoning. Cook another 2 minutes. Remove from heat and stir in the parsley and bread crumbs. Let the mixture cool. Mix in half of the beaten egg. Line 2 baking sheets with silicone-parchment paper. Preheat oven to 350°. Remove one half of the pastry from the refrigerator. Roll out on a lightly floured surface with a lightly floured rolling pin to ⅛-inch thickness. Cut into 3-inch rounds. Place 1 teaspoon of the meat mixture in the center of each round. Fold the rest of the pastry over to form a half-moon shape. Mix the rest of the beaten egg with the cream and seal the edges. Brush the top of each turnover with the egg-cream mixture. Prick with a fork. Place on the baking sheets. Use the same procedure with the other half of the pastry. Bake at 350° for 30 minutes. *Makes 36.*

Can be frozen. Freeze on aluminum foil pans, then place in plastic bags and seal. To serve, bake in a preheated 425° oven for 15 minutes.

TURNOVER SLICES

Unlike individual turnovers, turnover slices do not have to be separately shaped for each serving.

Make half the recipe for Cream-Cheese Pastry (see index). Wrap the dough in waxed paper and refrigerate 4 hours or overnight. Meanwhile, make your choice among the following fillings. When ready to use, let the dough stand at room temperature for 15 minutes. Cut the pastry into 2 pieces. Refrigerate half and work with the other half. Roll out on a lightly floured board with a floured rolling pin into a rectangle 14 inches long, 5 inches wide, and ⅛-inch thick. Line a baking sheet with silicone parchment paper. With the long side of the dough rectangle facing you, place 1 cup of the filling lengthwise along the center of the dough. Fold the long edge near you over the filling, covering about two thirds of the dough. Press along the edge. Brush the other long edge with the unbeaten white of 1 egg. Fold the third over and press to seal the roll. Place on the baking sheet seam side down. Refrigerate for 1 hour. Proceed with the other half of the dough in the same manner. Preheat oven to 350°. Cut each roll on an angle into 1-inch slices and separate slightly. Brush the top of the rolls with 1 egg beaten with 2 tablespoons heavy cream. Bake 30 minutes.

These can be reheated. Bake in a preheated 375° oven 5 to 7 minutes. *Makes about 28 slices.*

Can be frozen. Freeze on aluminum freezer trays, then cover the trays with plastic wrap and secure. To serve, bake unthawed in a preheated 375° oven for about 12 minutes or until heated through.

Italian Filling

3 tablespoons butter
½ cup finely chopped onion
1¼ cups prosciutto, shredded (5 ounces)
¼ pound mushrooms, thinly sliced
1 clove garlic, finely chopped (½ teaspoon)
¼ teaspoon freshly ground black pepper
1 10-ounce package frozen chopped spinach, thawed and drained
½ cup freshly grated Parmesan cheese
¼ cup pine nuts, toasted in a 350° oven for 8 minutes
1 cup pot cheese
2 eggs, beaten

In a medium-sized heavy skillet, melt the butter. Add the onion and prosciutto and sauté over medium heat 15 minutes. Add the mushrooms and garlic and sauté another 5 minutes. Add the pepper and remove from heat. Stir in the spinach, Parmesan cheese, pine nuts, and pot cheese. Cool slightly. Stir in the beaten eggs. *Fills about 28.*

Mexican Beef Filling

1½ tablespoons butter
½ cup minced onion
1 clove garlic, finely minced (½ teaspoon)
½ pound ground round beef
1 tablespoon chili powder
1 teaspoon dried oregano
½ teaspoon ground cumin seed
1 teaspoon salt
¼ teaspoon freshly ground black pepper
½ cup grated Cheddar cheese
2 tablespoons tomato paste
¼ cup chopped ripe olives
1 egg, lightly beaten

Melt the butter in a small skillet and sauté the onion and garlic until onion is softened but not brown. Add the meat and stir, breaking up the meat with a fork. Cook until the meat loses its red color. Add all remaining ingredients except the egg. Cook for a minute until the cheese melts. Remove from heat. Cool slightly, and then stir in the beaten egg. Cool, cover, and refrigerate for 1 hour. *Fills about 28.*

Smoked-Salmon Filling

2 teaspoons butter
2 teaspoons flour
½ cup heavy cream
1 tablespoon onion juice
¼ teaspoon cayenne pepper
¼ cup chopped fresh dill
½ pound smoked salmon, coarsely chopped (1 cup)
1 egg, lightly beaten

Melt the butter in a small, heavy saucepan. Off the heat, blend in the flour. Add the cream and onion juice gradually, stirring constantly. Return to heat and stir until the sauce is quite thick. Remove from heat and add the pepper and dill. Fold in the chopped salmon. Let cool for about 10 minutes. Stir in the egg. Chill the mixture, covered, for about 2 hours.

Spinach-Bacon Filling

6 slices bacon
1 small onion, finely chopped
2 cloves garlic, finely minced (1 teaspoon)
1 10-ounce package frozen chopped spinach,
    thawed and squeezed dry
1 cup pot cheese
½ teaspoon salt
¼ teaspoon freshly ground black pepper
⅛ teaspoon nutmeg
¼ cup finely chopped fresh dill.

Dice the bacon and sauté until crisp. Remove, drain on paper towels, and reserve. In the bacon fat remaining in the pan, sauté the onion and garlic until tender but not brown. Add the spinach and cook another minute. Stir in the remaining ingredients and add the reserved bacon. Cool, cover, and refrigerate for 1 hour.

CHINESE PORK-CRAB SLICES

Use Sour-Cream Pastry.

Sour-Cream Pastry

¼ pound (1 stick) cold butter
1¼ cups flour
pinch salt
½ cup sour cream

1 egg, separated
2 teaspoons heavy cream

In the large bowl of an electric mixer, cut the butter into the flour. Wrap a towel around the lip of the bowl to prevent spillage. Beat the mixture at low speed. Add the salt and sour cream and continue to beat until everything is incorporated. Divide the dough in half. Wrap halves in foil, flatten, and refrigerate 8 hours or overnight. Meanwhile, make the filling (see following recipe).

Remove the dough from the refrigerator. Roll out each half on a floured board to a rectangle about 12 inches by 5 inches and about ⅛-inch thick. Press the filling on the dough and roll from the long side, jelly-roll style. Brush the edges with the egg white to seal. Place the roll on an ungreased baking sheet and chill 1 hour. Preheat oven to 350°. Brush the top with the egg yolk beaten with the heavy cream. Bake 35 minutes. Let cool a bit. Cut into 1 inch slices. *Makes about 30.*

Can be frozen. Freeze in aluminum foil pans, then wrap in plastic bags and seal. To reheat, bake unthawed in a preheated 375° oven for about 12 minutes or until heated through.

Pork and Crab Filling

½ pound ground pork
½ cup cooked crabmeat
⅓ cup chopped water chestnuts
½ teaspoon salt
¼ cup scallions, chopped
2 teaspoons finely grated fresh ginger
1 tablespoon plus 1 teaspoon soy sauce
1 clove garlic, put through press (¼ teaspoon)
1 egg, beaten
2 tablespoons bread crumbs

In a skillet, cook the pork until it loses its pink color. Off the heat, add the rest of the ingredients. Cool.

HOMEMADE SAUSAGE IN PASTRY
(Saucisson en Croûte)

One thing I always order if I see it on the menu of a French restaurant is *saucisson en croûte*—that wonderful combination of brioche dough and garlic sausage. But French or Italian types of sausage are hard to find and brioche dough is time-consuming to make, so I devised this version. It does not have the rough texture of the original but the over-all flavor seems to delight everyone. Frozen, ready-made puff pastry is an excellent substitute for the brioche dough.

> 2 teaspoons bacon fat
> 1 large onion, minced (¾ cup)
> 1 pound ground pork
> 2 cloves garlic, finely chopped (1 teaspoon)
> 1 cup soft bread crumbs
> ¾ teaspoon salt
> ½ teaspoon dried sage
> ¾ teaspoon dried marjoram
> ¼ teaspoon dried oregano
> ¼ teaspoon dried thyme
> ⅛ teaspoon allspice
> ¼ teaspoon crushed bay leaf
> ¼ teaspoon dried, crushed red pepper
> 2 teaspoons fennel seeds
> 1 egg plus 1 egg yolk, lightly beaten
> ¼ cup chopped parsley
> 1 egg yolk beaten with 1 tablespoon water
> 2 sheets packaged puff pastry, 10 inches long by
>   5 inches wide

In a medium-sized skillet, melt the bacon fat and sauté the onion until it is golden. Add the pork and the garlic and continue to cook, breaking the meat up with a fork, for about 10 minutes or until the pork is gray and completely cooked. If the pork has let out fat, drain it off. Off the heat, add the bread crumbs, salt, sage, marjoram, oregano, thyme, allspice, bay leaf, red pepper, and fennel. Mix well. Let the mixture cool for about 10 minutes. Stir in the beaten egg and egg yolk and the chopped parsley. Chill the mixture for at least 2 hours. Preheat oven to 400°. Follow the instructions on the package of puff pastry, which require that it be thawed at room temperature for 10 minutes. On a piece of waxed paper, shape the meat mixture into a rectangle about 8 inches long and 2½ inches in diameter. Enclose the meat mixture in the waxed paper and squeeze it into a firm loaf. On a lightly floured surface, using a floured rolling pin, roll out each sheet of pastry until it it still 10 inches long but 6 inches wide. Put the meat roll on one sheet of the pastry and brush the edges with the egg yolk beaten with water. Place the other sheet of pastry on top and brush edges with the egg wash. Seal the loaf on all sides in the pastry. Place on an ungreased pastry sheet and brush the top with egg wash. Prick the top surface of the roll in several places with the tines of a fork. If there is more pastry than is needed to enclose the roll, cut out decorative shapes of flowers or leaves, place them on the brushed surface, and brush them with egg wash. Bake for about 25 minutes or until golden. Cool for 5 minutes and then cut into ¾-inch slices. Serve with small plates and forks. The roll may be made the day before and reheated; bake in a preheated 400° oven for 10 minutes. *Makes about 8 slices.*

Can be frozen. Freeze in a foil loaf pan, then place in a plastic freezer bag and seal. To serve, thaw overnight in the refrigerator and reheat as above.

Profiteroles

Most people associate profiteroles with the wonderful gooey dessert often served at elegant dinners. Surprisingly few know that the profiterole base, a cream puff, is one of the easiest pastries to prepare. Sogginess, its only pitfall, can easily be avoided if you follow the prescribed oven temperatures and baking times and slit the puffs while they are still hot so that the steam can escape. For the hors d'oeuvre tray they make marvelous cases for any creamed meat, fish, or vegetable combination, or cold salad mixture. They freeze beautifully, filled or unfilled, and you can keep a supply of unfilled puffs in the freezer to be recrisped in the oven.

COCKTAIL PROFITEROLES

These require Cream-Puff Pastry.

Cream-Puff Pastry

1 cup water
¼ pound (1 stick) butter, cut in 8 pieces
1 teaspoon salt
½ teaspoon dry mustard
1 cup flour
4 eggs

1 egg, beaten with 1 tablespoon heavy cream

Preheat oven to 425°. Lightly butter 2 baking sheets. In a saucepan over low heat, slowly bring to a full boil the water, butter, salt, and dry mustard. Off the heat, add the flour all at once, stirring vigorously with a wooden spoon. Return to low heat and beat the mixture until it leaves the sides of the pan and forms a ball. This usually takes about 2 minutes. Cool 3 minutes. Place in the mixing bowl of an electric mixer. Add the 4 eggs, one at a time, beating well after each addition. When all are added, beat 1 additional minute at high speed. Let cool 10 minutes. Spoon the paste into a pastry bag fitted with a no. 7 (½ inch) tube. Press the mixture out onto the lightly buttered baking sheets in mounds about 1½ inches in diameter. (Or shape puffs with spoons.) Leave about 2 inches between the puffs. Brush the top of each with the beaten egg and cream mixture. Bake in a preheated 425° oven for 15 minutes. Lower the heat to 350° and bake another 15 minutes without opening the oven door. Remove the puffs from the oven, turn heat off, and with a sharp knife poke a hole in the side of each puff. Return the puffs to the turned-off oven for 10 minutes. Remove and cool on a rack.

Make the filling (see following recipes). When puffs are cool, cut off part of the top to form a lid, fill, and replace lid. Reheat at 375° for about 10 minutes. *Makes 36.*

Can be frozen. Place on a flat surface to freeze, then pack in flat aluminum pans and seal securely. To serve, heat in a preheated 400° oven for 15 minutes.

Shrimp Filling

6 ounces cream cheese with chives
2 cups cooked tiny shrimp (20 ounces before shelling)
2 tablespoons fresh dill, finely chopped
2 tablespoons lemon juice
2 tablespoons grated onion
½ teaspoon salt
½ teaspoon white pepper
½ teaspoon Worcestershire sauce

Let the cheese soften to room temperature. Incorporate with remaining ingredients.

Curried Tuna Filling

1 6½-ounce can tuna fish, drained and flaked
1 ounce cream cheese
2½ teaspoons curry powder
¼ teaspoon salt
1 teaspoon grated onion
2 tablespoons chopped chutney
¼ cup roasted, diced almonds

Combine all ingredients.

German Filling

½ pound Liederkranz cheese
2 tablespoons butter
½ pound Black Forest ham or Westphalian ham,
    finely chopped (1⅓ cups)
½ teaspoon German mustard
6 tablespoons chopped chives
2 teaspoons caraway seeds

Soften the cheese and butter to room temperature. Stir in the other
ingredients.

Camembert Filling

1½ pounds Camembert cheese with rind
9 ounces cream cheese
6 slices bacon, cooked, drained and crumbled

Let the cheese soften to room temperature. Cream together and
stir in the bacon.

COCKTAIL GOUGÈRE

That glory of Burgundian pastry, *gougère*, a golden circle of cheese
puffs, dotted on the top with additional cheese, can also be reduced
to bite size.

Cream-Puff Pastry (see preceding recipe)
1 cup finely diced, unprocessed Gruyère cheese (⅜ pound)
1 egg, beaten with 1 tablespoon heavy cream
½ cup shredded, unprocessed Gruyère cheese (⅛ pound)

Make the pastry as directed but preheat oven to 375° instead of 425°. After all the eggs have been added, beat an additional minute at high speed, then fold in the diced Gruyère and make the puffs, leaving about 3 inches between them. Brush the tops with egg-cream mixture and sprinkle the tops with the shredded Gruyère. Bake for 25 minutes. Do not open the door. Meanwhile make the filling (see following recipes). When puffs are done, remove one and slit it across, ¼ inch from top, to be sure it is dry. Cool on a wire rack. Then slit the other puffs and fill. *Makes 36.*
Can be frozen. Freeze filled puffs on aluminum foil trays. Reheat from the frozen state at 375° for about 12 minutes.

Cheese Filling

1 cup grated Sap Sago cheese
1½ cups grated unprocessed Gruyère cheese (6 ounces)
¾ cup grated Muenster cheese
¾ cup butter, softened

Combine the grated cheeses and the softened butter.

Crabmeat or Shrimp Filling

2 cups crabmeat or shrimp
6 ounces cream cheese with chives
1 teaspoon salt
½ teaspoon pepper
2 tablespoons chopped chives
3 tablespoons chopped fresh tarragon or 1 teaspoon dried
2 tablespoons grated Parmesan cheese
1 clove garlic, minced (½ teaspoon)
¼ cup grated Gruyère cheese

Combine all the ingredients.

Quiches

Quiches, though now almost as common on menus as bacon and eggs, make such a delicious nibble that no hostess should overlook their potential for the hors d'oeuvre table. For this purpose, one-bite versions are preferable to wedges from a single large quiche, because they are easier to handle without benefit of plate or fork. The method I use for lining the tart pans eliminates the finicky business of rolling out the crust, cutting it, and carefully fitting it into a pan, and for these miniatures it is not necessary to bake the shells beforehand. You will find yourself improvising all sorts of additions to the basic custard filling, including many kinds of left-overs. These can all be frozen as explained in the first recipe.

MINIATURE QUICHES

    ¼ pound (1 stick) butter, at room temperature
    4 ounces cream cheese, at room temperature
    2 tablespoons heavy cream
    1¼ cups flour
    ½ teaspoon salt
    2 tablespoons melted butter

Cream the butter and cream cheese together thoroughly, using an electric mixer or food processor. Beat in the cream and then stir in the flour and salt until well mixed. Form the dough into a ball and wrap in waxed paper. Refrigerate at least 2 hours or overnight. With a pastry brush, generously grease 24 1-inch by ¾-inch muffin pans with the melted butter. Shape the dough into 24 1-inch balls.

Press dough evenly against the bottom and sides of each pan. Refrigerate while preparing filling. Fill and bake as in following recipe (Basic Lorraine Filling). Other recipes for fillings follow. *Makes 24.*

Basic Lorraine Filling

1 cup boiled ham, finely chopped
⅓ cup cooked bacon, finely crumbled
¼ cup finely grated Gruyère cheese
1 whole egg plus 1 additional yolk
¾ cup heavy cream
½ teaspoon salt
⅛ teaspoon cayenne pepper
⅛ teaspoon freshly grated nutmeg
⅓ cup freshly grated Parmesan cheese

Preheat oven to 425°. Distribute the ham and bacon on the bottom of the pastry cases. Sprinkle with the Gruyère cheese. In a small bowl, combine the egg, egg yolk, cream, salt, pepper, and nutmeg. Pour the mixture into the pastry cases and sprinkle the tops with Parmesan cheese. Bake 5 minutes. Reduce oven temperature to 350° and bake 20 minutes longer, or until the quiches are puffed and lightly browned on top. Cool on a rack for a few minutes. Carefully run a knife around the edges of each and turn out. Serve at once.

These can be made a day in advance and refrigerated overnight. Remove from the refrigerator ½ hour before serving. Preheat the oven to 375°. Place the quiches on a baking sheet and bake 10 minutes. *Fills 24.*

Can be frozen. Put the baked quiches on aluminum freezer trays and freeze, then seal the trays securely in plastic bags. To serve, remove from the freezer 1 hour before serving and heat as above.

Shrimp Filling

Substitute 1 cup cooked shrimp, coarsely chopped (about ¼ pound) for the ham and bacon, and 1 teaspoon chopped fresh dill and ½ teaspoon grated onion for the nutmeg. Proceed as before. *Fills 24.*

Smoked Salmon Filling

Omit the ham, bacon, Gruyère cheese, nutmeg, and Parmesan cheese. Sauté 2 tablespoons finely chopped onion in 1 tablespoon butter till transparent. Drain well. Place 1 cup coarsely chopped smoked salmon on the pastry. Combine the onion with the rest of the filling ingredients, and fill the pastry cases. Sprinkle the tops with 1 tablespoon chopped chives. Proceed as before. *Fills 24.*

Italian Sausage Filling

4 hot Italian sausages (about ¾ pound)
4 tablespoons scallions, finely chopped
2 cloves garlic, minced (1 teaspoon)
1 teaspoon Italian herb seasoning
1 teaspoon salt
6 ounces diced Fontina cheese
1 egg plus 1 additional yolk
¾ cup heavy cream
⅓ cup freshly grated Parmesan cheese

Remove the sausage from the casing and break up. Sauté in a medium-sized skillet until thoroughly cooked, about 15 minutes. Stir in the scallions and garlic and sauté another 5 minutes. Remove with a slotted spoon to a bowl. Add herb seasoning and salt. Place a few cubes of Fontina in the bottom of each pastry case. Add the sausage mixture. In a small bowl, combine the egg, egg yolk, and cream. Spoon into cases. Sprinkle the tops with Parmesan cheese.

Proceed as before. *Fills 24.*

Lobster or Crabmeat Filling

2 tablespoons butter
2 tablespoons chopped shallots
2 tablespoons chopped celery leaves
1 cup cooked lobster meat, preferably fresh, coarsely chopped (about ¼ pound), or 1 cup crabmeat, preferably fresh
¼ cup dry sherry

½ teaspoon salt
¼ teaspoon freshly ground black pepper
2 tablespoons chopped chives
½ teaspoon dried tarragon soaked in 1 tablespoon
   Pernod for 10 minutes
1 whole egg plus 1 additional yolk
¾ cup heavy cream
½ teaspoon salt
¼ teaspoon dry mustard
⅛ teaspoon cayenne pepper
⅓ cup grated Gruyère cheese

In a heavy skillet, melt the butter. Add the shallots and celery leaves. Sauté for about 4 minutes. Add the lobster meat or crabmeat, sherry, ½ teaspoon salt, and pepper. Sauté for a few minutes to evaporate the liquid completely. Add the chives and the soaked tarragon and cool the mixture. In a small bowl, combine the egg, egg yolk, cream, ½ teaspoon salt, dry mustard, and pepper. Spoon the lobster mixture into the bottom of the pastry cases. Cover with the custard mixture. Sprinkle grated Gruyère on top. Proceed as before. *Fills 24.*

Chicken-Liver Filling

6 tablespoons rendered chicken fat
2 large Spanish onions, chopped (4 cups)
4 cloves garlic, finely minced (2 teaspoons)
1 pound chicken livers
2 teaspoons salt
½ teaspoon freshly ground black pepper
2 tablespoons cognac
12 strips bacon, cooked and crumbled
¼ cup chopped parsley
1 whole egg plus 1 additional yolk
¾ cup heavy cream
½ teaspoon salt
⅛ teaspoon cayenne pepper
⅓ cup freshly grated Parmesan cheese

Melt the chicken fat in a heavy skillet and add the onions and garlic. Sauté until the onions are deep golden. Remove onions with a slotted spoon to a strainer. Add the livers to the remaining fat and sauté quickly until they are just pink in the center. This will take about 4 to 5 minutes. Add the 2 teaspoons salt, the black pepper, and the cognac and sauté another minute. Add these to the onion mixture in the strainer and drain for 10 minutes. Place the onions, livers, and bacon in a large chopping bowl. Chop to a fine paste. Stir in the parsley. Place a portion of the mixture in the bottom of each pastry case. In a small bowl, combine the egg, egg yolk, cream, ½ teaspoon salt, and the cayenne pepper. Spoon this custard mixture on top of the liver mixture, and sprinkle tops with the cheese. Proceed as before. *Fills 24.*

Mushroom Filling

4 tablespoons butter
4 tablespoons finely minced shallots
¾ pound fresh mushrooms, caps and stems, finely minced
2 tablespoons dry Madeira
1 teaspoon salt
½ teaspoon freshly ground black pepper
2 tablespoons chopped chives
⅓ cup chopped fresh dill
1 whole egg plus 1 additional yolk
¾ cup heavy cream

Melt the butter in a heavy medium-sized skillet. Add the shallots and sauté for about 3 minutes. Add the mushrooms and sauté, stirring often, for about 15 minutes. Add the Madeira and sauté until almost all the liquid has cooked away. Remove from heat. Add the salt, pepper, chives, and dill. Let the mixture cool ½ hour. Spoon into the cases. In a small bowl, combine the egg, egg yolk, and cream and spoon over the mushroom mixture.
Proceed as before. *Fills 24.*

MUSHROOM AND SMOKED-TURKEY FILLING
Use only 3 tablespoons shallots and ½ pound mushrooms. Omit the Madeira, black pepper, chives, and dill. Off the heat, add to

shallots and mushrooms ¼ pound smoked turkey, finely chopped (1 cup), 1 teaspoon dried tarragon, ¼ teaspoon salt, and a pinch of cayenne pepper. Cool. Place 1 teaspoon of the mixture in each pastry case. In a small bowl, combine the egg and egg yolk with ½ cup heavy cream, ½ teaspoon salt, ⅛ teaspoon cayenne pepper, and ⅛ teaspoon nutmeg. Spoon some of the custard mixture into each case. Sprinkle the tops with ½ cup grated Gruyère cheese. Proceed as before. *Fills 24.*

Clam Filling

36 pastry cases
2 8-ounce cans minced clams
2 teaspoons butter
2 tablespoons finely minced shallots
1 tablespoon arrowroot
½ teaspoon dry mustard
1 teaspoon dried oregano
1 teaspoon Worcestershire sauce
2 tablespoons chopped chives
2 tablespoons minced parsley
1 clove garlic, put through press (½ teaspoon)
½ teaspoon salt
pinch freshly ground black pepper
1 whole egg plus 1 additional egg yolk
¾ cup heavy cream
¼ cup grated Swiss cheese
paprika

Drain the clams. Reserve ¾ cup clam juice. Melt the butter in a small skillet and sauté the shallots until softened. Dissolve the arrowroot in the clam juice. Add to the shallots and stir over low heat until the mixture thickens. Combine drained clams, dry mustard, oregano, Worcestershire sauce, chives, parsley, garlic, salt, and pepper. Add to the shallot mixture. Put a portion of the mixture in the bottom of each pastry case. In a small bowl, combine the egg, egg yolk, and cream. Spoon over the clam mixture. Sprinkle the tops with grated Swiss cheese and paprika. Proceed as before. *Fills 36.*

ITALIAN EASTER PIES
(Piccolo Torta Rustica)

This simplified version of the traditional pie served in Italy at Eastertime retains all the savory ingredients but eliminates the drudgery of rolling out two crusts.

> 1 recipe Miniature Quiche pastry
> ½ pound sweet Italian sausage
> 2 ounces prosciutto, shredded
> 2 ounces Abruzzi sausage or Genoa salami, chopped
> 2 ounces mozzarella cheese, cut into ¼-inch dice
> 3 ounces grated Parmesan cheese
> 2 tablespoons chopped parsley
> ½ teaspoon salt
> ½ teaspoon freshly ground black pepper
> ½ cup ricotta cheese
> 1 egg
> 2 tablespoons butter, cut into 24 pieces

Make the pastry as directed. Preheat oven to 350°. Line 24 muffin pans with the pastry. Refrigerate. Remove the sweet sausage from the casing and sauté until it is no longer pink. Drain on paper towels. Put it into a mixing bowl and add the prosciutto, Abruzzi sausage or Genoa salami, mozzarella, 2 ounces of the Parmesan cheese, the parsley, salt, and pepper. Beat the ricotta cheese and the egg together until smooth. Combine with the sausage mixture. Put a generous teaspoonful in each pastry case. Sprinkle the remaining 1 ounce grated Parmesan cheese on the tops and put a dot of butter on each. Bake 35 minutes. *Makes 24.*
    Can be frozen.

ITALIAN TARTS
(Pissaladière San Remo)

> 1 recipe Miniature Quiche pastry
> 3 tablespoons olive oil
> 1½ cups finely chopped Bermuda onions

12 cloves garlic, chopped (2 tablespoons)
1 1-pound can tomatoes with tomato paste and basil,
  drained and chopped
2 tablespoons Italian herb seasoning
½ teaspoon salt
¼ teaspoon freshly ground black pepper
2 tablespoons grated Parmesan cheese
3 ounces Bel Paese cheese cut into 1-inch squares ⅛-inch thick
2 2-ounce cans anchovy fillets, drained, cut in half
6 Mediterranean olives, pitted and cut into quarters
2 tablespoons olive oil
2 tablespoons chopped parsley

Make the pastry as directed. Preheat oven to 350°. In a heavy, medium-sized saucepan, heat the olive oil. Add the onions and garlic and sauté slowly, covered, for about 30 minutes. Stir every 10 minutes. Do not let brown. Add the tomatoes and continue to cook slowly, uncovered, for another 20 minutes or until all the liquid has disappeared. Add the herb seasoning, salt, and pepper, and simmer 5 minutes more. Taste for seasoning; the mixture should be quite spicy.

Sprinkle the Parmesan cheese evenly on the bottom of each case. Spoon ½ teaspoon of the tomato-onion purée into each and top with a square of Bel Paese cheese. Crisscross anchovy halves on top and put an olive quarter in the center. Brush the tops with 1 tablespoon olive oil. Bake 30 minutes. Brush again, using the remaining 1 tablespoon olive oil. Sprinkle with chopped parsley. *Makes 24.*

Can be frozen. Freeze after baking on aluminum freezer trays, then seal securely in plastic bags. Remove from the freezer 1 hour before serving. Place on a baking sheet, brush with the second tablespoon olive oil, and bake in a preheated 375° oven for 10 minutes. Sprinkle with the parsley just before serving.

CRAB TARTS

Miniature Quiche pastry (see page 208)

DUXELLES
2 tablespoons butter
6 teaspoons finely chopped shallots
¼ pound mushrooms, finely chopped
¼ teaspoon salt
pinch cayenne pepper

CRAB FILLING
5 tablespoons butter
¼ cup finely minced scallions, white part only
¼ pound fresh crabmeat (1 cup)
½ teaspoon salt
¼ teaspoon white pepper
1 clove garlic, finely minced (½ teaspoon)
2 tablespoons dry Madeira
3 tablespoons finely chopped fresh dill
3 tablespoons flour
1 cup boiling clam juice
¾ cup grated Swiss cheese
1 egg yolk
¼ cup heavy cream
4 tablespoons melted butter

Make the pastry as directed. For the duxelles, melt the 2 table-spoons butter, add the shallots, and sauté for 5 minutes. Do not let them color. Add the mushrooms and cook for 10 to 15 minutes or until the liquid has evaporated. Remove from the heat and add the salt and cayenne pepper. Let cool and reserve.

To make the filling, melt 2 tablespoons of the butter in a skillet and sauté the scallions for 5 minutes. Add the crabmeat, salt, white pepper, garlic, and Madeira. Cook down until all the liquid has evaporated. Stir in the dill. In a heavy saucepan, melt the remaining 3 tablespoons butter. Add the flour and cook slowly for about 2 minutes. Off the heat, beat in the boiling clam juice. Return to heat and bring to a boil, whisking constantly. Stir in ¼ cup of the Swiss cheese. Beat the egg yolk with the cream.

Gradually pour a little of the hot sauce into the yolk-cream mixture, stirring constantly. Pour the mixture into the sauce and whisk to incorporate. Fold in the crabmeat mixture and the reserved duxelles. Taste for salt and pepper. Cool slightly.

Fill each pastry case with 1 generous tablespoon of the filling. Sprinkle the tops with the remaining ½ cup Swiss cheese. Drizzle about ⅛ teaspoon melted butter over each. Bake in a 350° oven for 35 minutes. *Makes 24*.

Can be frozen. Freeze the tarts on aluminum freezer trays, then seal the trays securely in plastic bags. Remove from freezer 1 hour before serving, place on a baking sheet, and bake in a preheated 375° oven for 10 minutes.

Phyllo

For years I had savored phyllo pastries in Greek restaurants, but not until I became a student in Ann Roe Robbins's cooking classes did I discover how easily I could reproduce them at home. Formerly, the strudel-like dough could be purchased only in a few Middle Eastern bakeries; now many supermarkets stock phyllo leaves in the dairy section. Properly wrapped, they will keep in your freezer for months. Phyllo is sold only in 1-pound packages, which contain 28 to 30 sheets, usually about 12 by 16 inches in size. Any not used at once can be frozen; defrost overnight in the refrigerator before using. Spinach and feta cheese or feta alone are the most common fillings, but many others are listed in Greek cookbooks.

As is true of many forbidding-sounding techniques, after you have once worked with a batch of phyllo, you will wonder why you had thought it difficult. The secret is not to let the leaves dry out while working and to be generous with the butter.

SPINACH-CHEESE TRIANGLES
(Spanakopetes)

    ½ pound phyllo leaves
    1 10-ounce package frozen chopped spinach
    3 tablespoons olive oil
    1 medium onion, finely chopped (about 1¼ cups)

¼ cup finely chopped scallions
½ pound feta cheese
¼ cup finely chopped parsley
¼ cup finely chopped fresh dill
½ teaspoon salt
¼ teaspoon freshly ground black pepper
pinch of freshly grated nutmeg
3 eggs, lightly beaten
½ pound butter, melted

If the phyllo leaves are frozen, thaw them overnight in the refrigerator. Thaw the spinach at room temperature (allow 3 to 4 hours). Drain off the water and squeeze the spinach in bunches between your hands to remove all the moisture. Heat the olive oil in a skillet and sauté the onion and scallions over medium heat until golden. Finely crumble the feta cheese in a large mixing bowl. Add the spinach, onion, scallions, parsley, dill, salt, pepper, nutmeg, and eggs. Combine well. Melt the butter.

Leave two-thirds of the ½ pound of phyllo in the refrigerator. Keep the third you are working with covered with waxed paper and a damp towel. Spread out additional waxed paper and remove 1 phyllo leaf. Cut into thirds. With a feathered brush, spread liberally with melted butter. Place 1 generous teaspoon of the spinach-cheese mixture in the bottom corner of the strip. Fold the pastry over so that the bottom edge meets a side edge and forms a right-angle triangle. Continue folding over from side to side into neat triangles until you reach the end of the strip. Brush the finished triangle with melted butter. Place on a jelly-roll pan (do not use a cookie sheet because the butter will run off the edge). Continue in this manner until all leaves have been used. When those in the refrigerator are needed, remove only half the remaining leaves at a time and keep all covered except the one you are working with.

Preheat oven to 400°. Bake 15 minutes or until golden. Cool 2–3 minutes before serving. *Makes about 24 triangles.*

Can be frozen. Freeze, unbaked, on a flat surface, then wrap carefully in a plastic bag and seal. To serve, place the frozen pastry on a sheet and bake at 400° for 25 to 30 minutes.

Lebanese Meat Filling

4 teaspoons butter
½ cup finely minced onion
1 clove garlic, finely minced (½ teaspoon)
½ pound ground beef
½ teaspoon cinnamon
½ teaspoon allspice
½ teaspoon freshly grated nutmeg
1 teaspoon salt
⅛ teaspoon freshly ground black pepper
4½ teaspoons tomato paste
1 tablespoon dried mint
1 teaspoon Escoffier Sauce Robert
½ pound phyllo leaves

Melt the butter in a medium-sized skillet. Add the onions and garlic and sauté for 3 minutes. Add the beef and while breaking it up with a fork cook only until it loses its red color. Remove from the heat. Add the remaining ingredients. Drain the mixture in a strainer for 5 minutes.

Prepare the phyllo leaves as for Spinach-Cheese Triangles. *Makes about 24.*

Crab Filling

2 6-ounce packages Alaska king crabmeat
2 teaspoons butter
2 tablespoons finely minced scallions
1 tablespoon flour
¼ cup milk
1 egg yolk, beaten
¼ teaspoon salt
¼ teaspoon freshly ground white pepper
pinch freshly grated nutmeg
¼ teaspoon dried oregano
1 teaspoon ouzo or anisette
1 tablespoon finely chopped Italian parsley
½ pound phyllo leaves

Defrost crabmeat overnight in the refrigerator. Drain, reserving ⅓ cup liquid. Squeeze out all the moisture and chop the crabmeat fine. Reserve. In a small, heavy saucepan, melt the butter and sauté the scallions 2 minutes. Add the flour and stir constantly over moderately high heat for 2 minutes. Add the milk and reserved crab liquid, and whisk until the sauce is smooth and thickened. Add a few tablespoons of the sauce to the beaten egg yolk and stir to heat yolk a bit, add to the sauce, and whisk just until it is incorporated. Remove from heat. Add the salt, pepper, nutmeg, oregano, ouzo, and parsley, and stir to combine. Add the chopped crabmeat and mix thoroughly.

Prepare phyllo leaves as for Spinach-Cheese Triangles. *Makes about 18.*

Italian Sausage Filling

½ pound Italian sweet sausage, removed from casings
1 tablespoon butter
1 cup chopped onion
1 clove garlic, minced (½ teaspoon)
¼ teaspoon freshly ground black pepper
¼ teaspoon salt
1 teaspoon dried basil
½ teaspoon dried oregano
1 tablespoon finely chopped Italian parsley

SAUCE
2 tablespoons butter
3 tablespoons flour
1 cup milk, scalded
2 egg yolks, well beaten
3 tablespoons freshly grated Parmesan cheese

½ pound phyllo leaves

In skillet, sauté the sausage until brown and cooked through. Keep breaking it up with a fork. Remove and drain on paper towels. In another skillet, melt the butter, and sauté the onion until transparent. Add the garlic for the last few minutes. Put the onions and sausage meat into a mixing bowl and add the salt, pepper, oregano, and chopped parsley. Mix well.

To make the sauce, melt the butter in a small, heavy saucepan, add the flour, and stir constantly with a wooden spoon for 2 or 3 minutes. Remove from heat, add the scalded milk, and stir with a whisk. Return to heat and whisk constantly until the sauce is thick and smooth. Add a few spoonfuls of the hot sauce to the egg yolks and beat to heat the yolks, then add to the sauce and whisk a minute. Add the cheese and cook just until the cheese melts. Combine with the meat mixture and cool.

Prepare phyllo leaves as for Spinach-Cheese Triangles. *Makes about 20.*

Chicken Filling

3 tablespoons butter
3 shallots minced (1 tablespoon)
¼ pound mushrooms, minced
2 tablespoons flour
½ cup chicken stock
pinch freshly ground white pepper
salt to taste (depending on the saltiness of the stock)
¼ teaspoon freshly grated nutmeg
1 egg yolk, beaten
¼ cup cream
2 tablespoons dry sherry
¼ cup grated Parmesan cheese
2 tablespoons minced parsley
1 cup cooked chicken, minced
3 tablespoons finely chopped black olives
1 pound phyllo leaves

In a small saucepan, melt the butter. Add the shallots, sauté for 1 or 2 minutes, and add the mushrooms. Sauté 5 minutes. Add the flour and stir with a whisk for about 3 minutes. Add the chicken stock and whisk over medium heat until the sauce thickens. Add the pepper, salt, and nutmeg. Combine the egg yolk and the cream in a small bowl. Add a bit of the hot sauce to the yolk mixture and stir well. Add the yolk mixture to the sauce. Add the sherry and cheese and heat, stirring, until the cheese melts. Take off the heat and add the parsley, chicken, and olives.

Prepare the phyllo leaves as for Spinach-Cheese Triangles. *Makes about 42.*

ANN ROE ROBBINS'S SHRIMP
IN EDIBLE PARCHMENT

1 pound jumbo shrimp (about 20)
2 slices lemon
3 tablespoons lime or lemon juice
6 tablespoons olive oil
½ teaspoon salt
¼ pound (1 stick) butter, melted
5 phyllo leaves
Sour-Cream Sauce (see following recipe)

Bring to a boil enough well-salted water to cover the shrimp, adding the lemon slices. Add the shrimp, unshelled, and cook for 5 minutes after the water has come to a boil again. Drain and shell. Make a marinade with the lime or lemon juice, olive oil, and salt. Add the hot shrimp and marinate at least until they have cooled. If they are to marinate more than 1 hour after cooling, cover with plastic wrap and refrigerate. Preheat oven to 350°.

As always, when using phyllo, work with only 1 leaf at a time and work as quickly as possible. Brush the leaf with melted butter. Cut into 4 long strips. Place a shrimp near the top of each and add ½ teaspoon Sour-Cream sauce. Fold the top end of the leaf over the shrimp, and then fold in the sides. Brush with melted butter. Roll up, brushing with butter. Place on a jelly-roll pan. Chill for ½ hour or as long as overnight. Bake in a 350° oven about 15 minutes or until golden brown. Serve hot with Duck Sauce or hot Mustard Sauce (see index). *Makes about 20.*

SOUR-CREAM SAUCE

½ cup sour cream
½ cup mayonnaise
1 teaspoon dry mustard
1 tablespoon lemon juice
1 teaspoon grated onion
¼ cup finely chopped fresh dill
1 teaspoon salt

Blend all the ingredients together and chill, covered, for at least 3 hours but preferably overnight.

This sauce is also excellent with cold poached shrimp. *Makes enough for 1½ pounds shrimp.*

Survival Kit
for Emergencies

It happens to everybody: people drop by just at the cocktail hour or, having spent the afternoon, seem reluctant to leave. Naturally you offer such guests a drink, which you feel you must supplement with some tidbit less banal than peanuts or pretzels. All too often, these occasions occur when your freezer bank balance is low. You don't want to make a production of dashing back and forth to pop things in and out of the oven, so this is the time when your refrigerator and emergency ration shelves must come to your rescue. If you keep replenishing supplies, such drop-ins will cause no problems.

Keep your eyes open for the new items that are constantly being offered to help the hurried hostess. Recently guacamole has appeared in the frozen food section of supermarkets; stuffed grape leaves and baby eggplants are stocked in the so-called gourmet food department; and I have even found the sesame dip, *hummus bi tahini*. Admittedly, the hors d'oeuvres you prepare from scratch are more interesting, but the quickies suggested in this section make acceptable substitutes when minutes count.

Refrigerator, Freezer, and Pantry Shelves

These lists are not meant to be definitive, but only to suggest items you will find helpful to keep on hand and where to store them. Those for pantry shelves are of course in packages, cans, or jars.

IN THE REFRIGERATOR
  carrots
  celery
  fresh dill
  garlic
  onions
  fresh parsley
  scallions
  lemons
  eggs
  butter or margarine
  sour cream
  cream cheese
  long-keeping natural cheeses: Cheddar, Monterey jack, Swiss,
    provolone, Gouda, blue cheese; Camembert and Brie in
    cans
  Parmesan cheese
  processed cheese spreads
  mayonnaise
  Dijon mustard
  horseradish
  anchovy paste
  bottled salad dressings

IN THE FREEZER
    cocktail pumpernickel
    cocktail rye bread
    Italian bread
    Frozen patty shells
    Brown-and-serve rolls
    Fried shrimp, crab balls, fish bites
    mini-pizzas
    Shrimp Newburg
    egg rolls
    cocktail franks in pastry
    ice cream

ON THE PANTRY SHELVES
    bacon bits
    catchup
    olive oil
    vegetable oils
    Escoffier Sauce Diable and Sauce Robert
    soy sauce
    Tabasco
    red and white wine vinegars
    Worcestershire sauce

    cayenne pepper
    chili powder
    curry powder
    dill weed
    dry mustard
    Italian herb seasoning
    oregano
    tarragon
    thyme
    other herbs and spices of your choice

    anchovies
    antipasto: artichoke hearts, caponata, olives, peppers
    artichoke bottoms and hearts
    canned ham

canned sausages and frankfurters
cannelini beans
caviar
chick peas
crabmeat
deviled ham
Fondue or cheese soup
Greek stuffed grape leaves
herring
meatballs
meat spreads
mushroom caps and pieces
olives, stuffed, ripe pitted, garlic, oil-cured, Greek
pâtés
pickled vegetables: eggplant, beans, beets, peppers,
    onions, cauliflower, tiny stuffed eggplant
quenelles or Scandinavian fish balls
roasted red peppers
sardines
shrimp
tuna fish
chili
corned beef hash
tomato-meat spaghetti sauce
clam sauce
Scandinavian crisp breads
English water crackers
Melba toast
potato chips
corn chips
bread sticks
sesame crackers
wheat crackers
canned pumpernickel
pasta
rice
potato sticks
cookies

SOUPS:
black-bean
clam chowder
cream of mushroom
gumbo
minestrone
onion
shrimp and lobster bisque
split-pea

Cocktail Quickies

MELBA TOAST

This is a good way to use up bread that is about to get stale.

Use thin-sliced white bread. This is a good basic bread to have on hand. Trim off the crusts and cut the slices in half or into triangles. Bake in a preheated 250° oven for 30 minutes. Can be stored in an airtight container for a few weeks or can be frozen.

MELBA ROUNDS
Preheat oven to 350°. With a round 1½-inch cutter, cut 4 rounds from each slice of bread. Brush with melted butter. Bake 7 minutes. (12 slices bread and ½ cup melted butter makes 48 rounds.)

SKEWERED TIDBITS

COLD
Cubes of salami or ham, cubes of cheese, slices of pickle or olives; cubes of ham with pickled onions.

BROILED
Cocktail franks, split, and spread with Cheddar cheese spread.
Canned mushroom caps and split cocktail franks, brushed with melted butter mixed with a little Dijon mustard.
Cubes of canned pineapple and ham, brushed with maple syrup.

Canned cocktail meatballs, cocktail onions, and stuffed olives, brushed with garlic butter.

BROILED CANAPÉS

Place any of the following on cocktail bread or crackers and put under the broiler.

Slice of salami and Cheddar cheese.
Slice of ham and Swiss cheese.
Sardine with whipped cream cheese and minced onion.
Tuna, chopped scallions, mayonnaise, and Cheddar cheese.
Deviled ham with Swiss or Cheddar cheese.
Sharp Cheddar cheese spread with bacon bits (real or imitation).
Cheddar cheese spread with Chutnut or chutney.
Crackers or cocktail salty rye slices, covered with a slice of mozzarella and a dot of anchovy paste.

COLD VEGETABLES

Raw mushroom caps filled with Boursin cheese.
Anchovy fillets wrapped around red radishes.
Tiny stalks of raw asparagus wrapped in a slice of prosciutto or boiled ham spread with Dijon mustard.
Pickled vegetables: beans, cauliflowers, carrot sticks, brussels sprouts, baby corn. Sprinkle with finely chopped parsley or dill. Drain and serve with picks.
Canned artichoke hearts and pitted ripe olives in vinaigrette or a ready-made vinegar and oil dressing.
Canned artichoke hearts or bottoms filled with canned liver spread or pâté or cheese spread and broiled.
Canned vegetable mixture—mushrooms, asparagus, artichoke hearts, baby carrots, green beans, or hearts of palm—with oil and vinegar dressing, sprinkled with chopped parsley.

Cannellini beans, drained, rinsed, and tossed with bottled oil and vinegar dressing or homemade vinaigrettte dressing, with a sprinkling of chopped scallions on top. For a more substantial dish, mix in a can of Italian tuna fish.

FISH

Canned or bottled gefilte fish balls attached to a cabbage with toothpicks. Hollow out the center of the cabbage and fill the cavity with a small bowl holding horseradish.

Canned Icelandic trout—serve with mustard or lemon mayonnaise.

Canned fillets of mackerel in white wine, with lemon wedges.

Smoked sprats with lemon wedges and buttered brown bread.

Smoked trout with horseradish sauce.

Quenelles or fish balls heated in cream of mushroom soup or lobster or shrimp bisque, laced with a little dry sherry.

Canned mussels, drained and heated in an herb butter.

Dried shrimp chips fried for 30 seconds.

Anchovies, roasted red peppers, and ripe olives tossed with oil and vinegar dressing to which chopped garlic, a pinch of oregano, and/or chopped parsley may be added.

Codfish balls made from a canned mixture and served with chili sauce spiked with horseradish, Tabasco, or Tartare Sauce.

Sardines on toasted fingers of white bread, crusts removed, topped with a squirt of lemon juice and some chopped parsley.

Sardine spread: Soften 1 3-ounce package cream cheese with chives to room temperature; add 3 4⅜-ounce cans boneless sardines, (skin on), 2 tablespoons lemon juice, 3 tablespoons grated onion, 12 dashes Angostura bitters, and 5 dashes cayenne pepper; and blend. *Makes 1½ cups.*

Can be frozen, and thawed overnight in the refrigerator.

MEAT

Prosciutto or Westphalian ham wrapped around melon cubes, pineapple chunks, figs, or canned pears.

Canned mushroom caps filled with deviled ham and broiled, or
filled with braunschweiger or pâté and baked to heat through.
Decorate with a slice of pimiento-stuffed olive. Or stuff with
canned shrimp mixed with curry mayonnaise.

Deviled ham or chicken spread mixed with curry mayonnaise to fill
celery sticks or canned mushrooms or as a spread for crackers.

Corned beef spread mixed with mustard mayonnaise and used in
the same way.

Liverwurst spread mixed with canned bacon bits and some curry
mayonnaise.

Melba Rounds covered with rounds of salami or ham, topped with
grated cheese, and broiled until the cheese melts.

Turkey cubes dipped into curry mayonnaise and then into chopped
peanuts or toasted almonds.

CHEESE COMBINATIONS

Cheddar cheese spread combined with chili powder, dabbed on corn
chips, and broiled 1 minute.

Cream cheese mixed with anchovy paste, minced onion, Italian
herb seasoning, chili, curry powder, or any spice you prefer:
spread on Melba Rounds and broiled for 1 or 2 minutes or until
the top browns slightly.

Quick pizzas—refrigerator biscuits topped with prepared pizza
sauce, a few pinches of oregano, some shredded cheese (preferably mozzarella), and an anchovy or dab of anchovy paste,
or a slice of salami or pepperoni or some canned sliced mushrooms. Bake according to package directions for biscuits.

Grated cheese or onion, chili, or garlic powder heated with pop-
corn, potato chips, or canned potato sticks.

Hasty Pastry

Refrigerator canned biscuits and rolls, of which supermarkets stock various types, can easily be filled and baked to provide pastry cases in a hurry. The fillings given in this section may be used interchangeably or you can utilize leftovers or the jars or cans on your shelves to create others. Remember, anything enclosed in pastry should be spicy and piquant. Filled refrigerator biscuits and rolls can be baked in the morning and reheated; cover loosely with foil and bake at 350° for 10 minutes.

BISCUIT TURNOVERS

Split biscuits in half. With the back of your fist flatten the dough and place about a teaspoon of the desired filling in the center. Fold the dough over to enclose the filling and press the edges together. These can be baked flat or set with edges up, looking like little boats. Bake them as the package directs, but check during the last few minutes; often the times on the package are a bit too long for these miniatures.

Curried Tuna Filling

1 3½-ounce can tuna fish
3 tablespoons finely chopped scallions
2 tablespoons mayonnaise
1½ teaspoons curry powder

236

Drain the tuna fish and put it in a small bowl. With a fork, break it into small pieces. Add the scallions. In a separate bowl, combine the mayonnaise and curry powder. Combine with the tuna mixture. Put 1 teaspoon filling in each half biscuit. *Fills about 10 biscuits, which means 20 pieces.*

Deviled Ham Filling

1 4½-ounce can deviled ham
1 teaspoon grated onion
4 teaspoons minced sweet gherkins
2 tablespoons mayonnaise
½ teaspoon Dijon mustard

Combine the ham, onion, and gherkins. Mix the mayonnaise with the mustard and combine with the ham mixture. Use 1 teaspoon for each turnover.

VARIATION
Combine the deviled ham with 2 tablespoons Duck Sauce and ¼ teaspoon grated fresh ginger.

Other Suggested Fillings

Small cubes of salami, cubed ham with a sprinkling of sharp Cheddar cheese, chopped chicken livers, braunschweiger, sardines with a sprinkling of lemon juice, or a good cheese spread.

BUTTERFLAKE ROLL TARTS

Use tartlet pans 1¾ inches wide and 1 inch deep. Place two leaves in each pan, one on top of the other, fitting them in to cover the entire surface. Fill and bake at 375° for 20 minutes.

Anchovy Filling

½ cup whipped cream cheese
1 teaspoon anchovy paste
2 teaspoons grated onion

Combine and fill tarts. *Makes 12 tarts.*

CANNED CRESCENT TRIANGLES

1 8-ounce can refrigerated crescent rolls
2 eggs
¼ pound ground ham (1 cup)
¼ pound grated sharp Cheddar cheese (1 cup)
2 teaspoons Dijon mustard
1 tablespoon heavy cream

Unroll the packaged dough and separate into the 8 portions marked by the perforations. Cut each in half on the diagonal. Beat 1 of the eggs and mix in the ham, cheese, and mustard. Place ½ teaspoon of the mixture in the center of each triangle, fold over the other half, and press to seal. Beat the remaining egg with the cream, and lightly brush the surface of each triangle. Place the filled pastries on an ungreased baking sheet and bake in a 375° oven for 12 to 13 minutes, or until golden brown. *Makes 16.*

Recycled
Leftovers

Leftover vegetables, fish, or meat, too often relegated to a dark corner of the refrigerator only to be thrown out later, can be retrieved to make a variety of hors d'oeuvres. In the earlier sections of this book there are many recipes that require only a bit of cooked food; keep these in mind in connection with leftovers.

SPREADS AND NIBBLES

A few general suggestions for converting different kinds of leftovers.

Small quantities of different cheeses: grate together and mix with a little butter, a few drops of whiskey or cognac, and seasoning.

Bits of fish or meat: mix with grated onion, herb or curry seasoning, and mayonnaise for a spread or a filling for toast cups.

Vegetables, cooked or raw: marinate in Vinaigrette Sauce or seasoned mayonnaise. Serve with toothpicks.

Ham: cube; spear each on a toothpick with a pineapple chunk and dip into Curry Mayonnaise.

Beef: cube; spear with a cocktail onion or a pickle.

Chicken: cube; spear with half a black olive, and dip into Tarragon Mayonnaise.

Pork: cube and heat; serve with Guacamole.

Fish: cube; serve with cocktail sauce, Green Goddess Sauce, or Mustard Mayonnaise.

CRISPY POTATO PEELS

A mystery hit at any party. When you are baking potatoes to use the cooked flesh in another dish, hoard the peels in the freezer, and defrost them in the refrigerator overnight. Or bake the potatoes for this and reserve the insides. Warning: never bake potatoes in foil (in which they are often sold) or you will have steamed potatoes.

> baked potato skins
> melted butter
> salt
> chopped chives
>
> TOPPINGS (optional)
> whipped cream cheese
> Grated sharp Cheddar cheese

Cut the skins into 1-inch strips. Brush both sides with melted butter. Salt the inner surface and sprinkle the chives on it. You can also spread the inner surface with whipped cream cheese and sprinkle with additional chives or spread with grated Cheddar cheese. Bake in a preheated 400° oven for 5 minutes.

NEW ENGLAND PÂTÉ

This savory pâté utilizes the remains of the traditional New England boiled dinner; well-seasoned store-bought corned beef can also be used. With a food processor, this can be assembled in less than 5 minutes; even with a meat grinder, it takes very little longer.

> ½ pound corned beef, cut into 1-inch chunks
> 6 tablespoons butter, at room temperature
> 2 tablespoons grated onion
> 2 teaspoons Dijon mustard
> 2 tablespoons minced parsley
> 2 teaspoons Escoffier Sauce Robert
> 1 teaspoon horseradish
> 1 teaspoon salt

Coarsely grind the meat in a food processor or meat grinder. Combine all the ingredients in a bowl and mix thoroughly. Pack into a 2-cup loaf pan or decorative bowl. Chill overnight or up to 2 days. When ready to serve, decorate the surface with gherkin fans. Serve with thin, narrow slices of pumpernickel, preferably the German type. *Makes 2 cups, about 15 slices if made in loaf.*

SMOKED TURKEY PÂTÉ

The remnants of the smoked turkey you served at your last gala buffet can be salvaged for still another party.

½ pound smoked turkey, cut into 1-inch chunks
3 tablespoons chopped shallots
3 tablespoons softened butter
¼ cup flour
2 tablespoons heavy cream
2 tablespoons Madeira
2 eggs
1 teaspoon Dijon mustard
1 teaspoon prepared horseradish
1 teaspoon dried tarragon
Mustard-Cheese Rosettes (see following recipe)

Preheat oven to 350°. Put the turkey pieces into the bowl of a food processor and run the machine for 2 minutes or until the turkey is finely ground. Add the rest of the ingredients and process for another minute to combine. Or grind the turkey pieces fine in a meat grinder, put into a bowl, add the other ingredients, and mix thoroughly. Spread the mixture in a greased 1½-cup loaf pan. Cover securely with heavy foil. Place the pan in a baking dish and pour boiling water around the pan to reach halfway up the side. Bake 50 minutes. Remove and cool. Cover with foil or plastic wrap and refrigerate overnight. To serve, turn out onto a platter and decorate with Mustard-Cheese Rosettes. Serve with whole-wheat melba toast. *Makes 1½ cups, about 10 slices.*

Mustard-Cheese Rosettes

¼ pound cream cheese, at room temperature
1 teaspoon Dijon mustard

Work the mustard into the softened cream cheese. If desired, add a drop of yellow food coloring. Using a pastry bag with a No. 3 tube, pipe rosettes around the top edge of the pâté.

Suppers
for Lingerers

Even though invitations read "Cocktails—Five to Seven," at nine o'clock there are often a few hardy survivors. At this point, the gracious course is to produce a light supper. Even if the refrigerator is pretty well cleaned out, the emergency shelf can yield quick, tasty, and substantial fare.

CANNED SOUPS ENHANCED

Black-bean soup heated with a shot of sherry and topped with sliced hard-cooked eggs or croutons.
Minestrone heated with extra canned tomatoes to thicken.
Onion soup heated with a dash of red wine and topped with French bread slices covered with melted cheese.
Split-pea soup heated with chunks of ham or frankfurters.
Gumbo soup heated with canned crabmeat.

MAIN DISHES

PASTA: cook and serve piping hot with heated canned tomato meat sauce or clam sauce, plus a pinch of herbs.
Canned chili heated and served with corn chips.
Canned fish balls heated in shrimp or lobster bisque and served on heated frozen patty shells or rice.

JIFFY CRAB NEWBURG: mix canned crabmeat and canned cream of mushroom soup thinned with a few tablespoons of heavy cream and spiked with sherry. Heat through and serve in heated frozen patty shells or with rice.

CANNED MEATBALLS: heat in spaghetti sauce and serve over pasta.

COLD PLATTER: salami, pepperoni, and other cold cuts, with cheeses (Swiss, Cheddar, Provolone, Gouda).

SEAFOOD PLATTER: sardines, salmon, tuna fish, crabmeat, and mussels, served with lemon wedges, chopped scallions, and mayonnaise.

ACCOMPANIMENTS

SALAD BAR: fill a bowl with whatever salad greens you have on hand and surround it with small dishes containing a selection (depending on your supplies) of anchovies, artichoke hearts, asparagus, bacon bits, beets, chick-peas, green beans, cubes or slivers of ham, olives, hearts of palm, mushrooms, fresh onion slices, pimientos, tuna fish, cubes or slivers of cheese, croutons. Serve with a choice of dressings.

Platter of canned vegetables, drained and drizzled with oil and vinegar.

Heated brown-and-serve rolls (if starch is lacking in the menu).

DESSERTS

Ice cream, if your freezer can provide it.
Packaged cookies.
Lots of coffee.

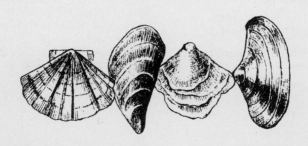

Index